THE
DIARY OF A
FREED MASON

A
Christian Viewpoint of
Freemasonry

David W. M. Vaughan

Sovereign

"But you are a chosen race, a royal priesthood, a holy nation, a people for God's own possession, that you may proclaim the excellencies of Him Who has called you out of darkness into His marvellous light;"   I Peter 1 v 9

Sovereign World Ltd
P.O. Box 17
Chichester
England PO20 6RY

Bible references are from the New American
Standard Bible Copyright © The Lockman
Foundation 1960, 1962, 1963, 1968, 1971, 1973, 1975,
1977 unless otherwise stated.

Scripture quotations marked NIV are from the Holy
Bible, New International Version Copyright © 1973,
1978, International Bible Society

Published by Hodder & Stoughton

Typeset by M R Reprographics, 42 High Street,
Chard, Somerset TA20 1QS

ISBN 1 85240 006 4

Printed and bound in England by Anchor Brendon
Ltd, Tiptree, Essex

Contents

Prologue

ONE Monday evening in the middle of April, 1979, a friend rang from London to tell me that the inaugural dinner of the Ipswich Chapter of the Full Gospel Business Men's Fellowship International was to take place on the following Friday and urged me to attend. I had read one or two books in which I had noticed the initials F.G.B.M.F.I., but was uncertain as to what took place during their meetings. John was persistent and excited. I agreed finally, contacted the secretary and booked a place.

On my arrival at the hotel I was thrilled to meet a number of friends from differing walks of life accompanied by their wives. They told me quite bluntly that I ought to have brought Mary, my wife, along with me and that I was to bring her to the next month's function. That evening was a new kind of experience for me and so enjoyable that I took Mary along to the May meeting. We were both so happy and uplifted on that occasion that we have gone on to be present at virtually every F.G.B.M.F.I. meeting held in Ipswich to date. Soon I was accepted as a member and nearly three years later, the other members honoured me by appointing me as their president. This position I am privileged to have held for the past four years.

This Fellowship publishes a magazine called "VOICE" every two months. It contains some half-a-dozen testimonies of business men who share what Jesus has done in their lives. The local director of the F.G.B.M.F.I. had asked me several times to submit my own testimony to the editor for publication. Significantly I had no urge to do this sort of thing until well into the autumn of 1983. I submitted a script which after being edited duly appeared in the second issue for 1984. The cover was so appropriate from my point of view for it featured a couple of parachutists in free-fall over the caption:- "SET FREE".

My copies of "VOICE" arrived by the second post on a Friday. On the following Monday morning a Minister telephoned from outside the United Kingdom. He explained that there were several Freemasons in his congregation and he was receiving little response or cooperation from them; could I help or advise him in any way? After some correspondence I received a letter thanking me for the help that I had been able to extend to him. I thank God for His guidance, for I had no first hand knowledge of the details of this Minister's situation; nor did I realise that this was just the beginning. God is so loving and caring; He leads His children step by step, day by day. Would I have sent a brief resume of my testimony to "Voice" if I had known where it would lead? "Voice" has a wider circulation than I had first appreciated!

Chapter 1

Beginnings

AS I write I am sitting in our "Upper Room" some sixteen feet by twenty-three feet, an extension to a compact three bedroomed house on a modern housing estate.

A couple of years ago the Lord guided us to sell our small farm, "Walnut Tree", and move. My wife and I had no idea where we were to go, but we did think that He wanted us to stay somewhere in Suffolk. Mary read advertisements in the local newspapers and together we visited a few estate agents. After spending nearly an hour in the third agent's office we were on the point of leaving when the manager called us back. He had remembered a house which the owner had taken off the market some six months earlier unable to sell it. Thinking it might interest us he suggested that he would check up and, if it were still for sale, would make an appointment to view. This he did.

Later, sitting outside the house in the car with Mary I remember so clearly agreeing with her that this was certainly not the house for us. Our little farmhouse was isolated, no papers were delivered and we fetched our milk from the milking parlour a mile or so away. Our only connections with the outside world were electricity, telephone and when the postman called. We even had our own well some hundred and thirty feet deep under the house. We had envisaged a house in one of the small lovely East Anglian villages with a few shops near and handy to make life a little easier and here we were in the middle of a new housing estate. However, no sooner had my wife put her foot inside the door when she turned to me and said:-

"This is the place".

Also, as soon as I had entered the house I knew that this was the house that the Lord had in mind for us. Upstairs the house was being altered quite dramatically; three or four days earlier and we would have been very doubtful, a few days later and our answer would have been an emphatic negative for what is now our "Upper Room" was about to be converted into a "granny flat". All the necessary building materials were already stacked up in the room when we viewed it. Since then God has given us a number of assurances that we are in the right place in His Will.

Recently a dear friend had died whilst making a speech at a Masonic banquet. He had sung in the church choir where I had been organist. We had been Freemasons together for a number of years although members of different Lodges. After my resignation from "The Craft", I had been unable to convince him why, as a Christian, I had had to re-nounce Freemasonry - and now he was dead. Many Freemasons attended his funeral, some I had known quite well, but now it seemed that they did not want to know me.

A week after the cremation whilst reading one of

my favourite authors - Colin Urquhart - the Lord indicated to me that I was to stop reading books and turn exclusively to His Word, the Bible. Without a qualm I closed the book, and was quite happy to put it back on the shelf although I was at an exciting passage.

A couple of days later I received a suggestion that I should write a book on the Christian view of Freemasonry. Now a short testimony in VOICE is one thing, it had taken years to persuade me to do even that; but to actually write a book was completely outside my ideas and capabilities.

Recovering from this daunting prospect I began to realise the urgency and appropriate timing of the project. Such a book must be written and as it seemed that God had been preparing me for the task then He would provide all that was necessary. My testimony would not fill a book, hardly form a reasonable chapter and I could think of only a couple of "Freedmasons" who might be able to help. This book could not be written by me, not by me alone, but God is in control!

As I was obedient in taking the first steps, then my Heavenly Father provided for the next. On a journey down from London another ex-Mason's name - Ronald Price - came to mind. We had met briefly at the 1983 National Convention of the F.G.B.M.F.I. at Blackpool. Upon my return home I contacted him by telephone. Yes, he was interested, and would help me in every way possible. What a boost that was for me! Also, Ron was due to speak at a nearby F.G.B.M.F.I. dinner in a few days time and could easily visit me. Thus it began,

3

and slowly more people came to mind. It is God Who is putting this book together and it is the assurance of His faithfulness that has given me the strength and determination to carry on.

Chapter 2

Into Freemasonry

SOME twenty years ago I was a member of five masonic lodges. Part of me enjoyed most of their assemblies. The brethren with whom I sat in Lodge were great people. Their friendship, encouragement and caring combined to make lodge meetings and lodge rehearsals very pleasant affairs. Notwithstanding, I had disquiet over the horrendous masonic obligations - that is the oaths binding one to maintain the secrecy of the Craft - but as church dignitaries, Bishops and Archbishops, as well as Kings and Dukes had been initiated into Freemasonry, who was I to object?

As well as being a Freemason I was also deeply involved in spiritualism - spiritism may be a better term - developing as a medium and had made an incursion into yoga. All these, I now realise, were occult activities. Yet I had been brought up to be a church-goer. I had been a churchwarden of a daughter church for over ten years, played the organ, taught in the local Sunday school and had been secretary and treasurer to the Parochial Church Council - but perhaps I ought to go back to the beginning.

When I was born, my Father was on active service with the Royal Navy in the Mediterranean area and I was some three years old before we met. This, I suppose, was the reason why I found it difficult to relate to him, especially when a brother arrived on the scene a couple of years later, and then eighteen months later a sister. This awkwardness between us persisted to some degree until, in his later years, we began to make up for lost time.

My Father was a great man, I came to admire him tremendously, his word was his bond. However, he was a Freechurchman, my Mother's parents were staunch Anglicans. Consequently, as a child I was very rarely taken to any place of worship.

May I digress for a moment? It was only after I had written the first draft of this book that I realised that I did not know when I had been 'born again' so I asked Jesus to show me when it was that I had asked Him to be Lord of my life. He immediately revealed to me that it was when I was quite young.

When about six years of age I went off on my own one evening to a very small chapel, which was near my home, to see a "magic lantern" show - I had never seen one before. Of all my childhood memories this event is easily the most vivid, not because of the novelty of seeing such large pictures on the screen, but for two succeeding slides which are as clear to me to-day as if I had seen them last week. Even the "wigging" I received when I returned home late fades into insignificance. These are the only scenes that I can remember from the entire evening. The first one showed "Christian" from John Bunyan's "Pilgrim's Progress" struggling up a hill with a colossal black trunk of a burden strapped on his back. The next picture was almost identical except that the burden was now lying on the ground at his heels with the straps broken. What the commentator said at this juncture I have no idea, but the memory of these two frames remains with astonishing clarity. Then I remembered that I had said that such a release from bondage was what I wanted. Thus not really knowing the implications of spiritual life, Jesus has been my Lord all these years.

This revelation instantly resolved one query that had bothered me for years. Almost invariably if I had entered a room in which a heated discussion, or even a full blown row was in progress, it would cease. I can remember an occasion when, at the last production meeting that I attended before my retirement, one of my colleagues turned to me and said that he was going to do something that I was not going to like, he was going to swear. He did. It concerned me that an apology was tendered at all, let alone in advance. This same influence was noticeable even when I was in the Royal Air Force. Now I realise that it was nothing to do with me at all, but somehow the other people had recognised Jesus in me. It is doubtful if they would have expressed it in this way, I certainly did not appreciate the truth of the situation until now. But to return to my story .....

Approaching the age of sixteen my Godparents decided that it was about time for me to be confirmed into the Church of England. If this would make everybody happy I was agreeable. Although not fond of public ceremonies, if this would lead me to know more about Jesus then I was all for it. Along with a group of children, mainly young girls of around twelve years of age, I was duly presented to the Bishop of Stafford. My preparation had been minimal, and I remember feeling rather "cissy" about the whole affair.

I closed my eyes when the Bishop laid his hands upon my head and prayed:-

"Defend, O Lord this Thy child with
Thy heavenly grace, that he may continue
Thine for ever, and daily increase in Thy
Holy Spirit, more and more, until he come
to Thine everlasting kingdom".

I said "Amen" and meant it!

What was I going to see when I opened my eyes? This had not been mentioned to me during the confirmation classes. The possibility of seeing God, or Jesus, was really too much for me, but maybe an angel - or even two? Cautiously opening my eyes I could see no change at all. I felt distinctly disappointed, somehow let down. At the close of the ceremony, as I was trying to sort this out in my own mind, someone asked me if I felt different. I didn't and said so rather pointedly. I felt let down, disillusioned! I did not realise then that one should rely on the Word of God, what He has said, and not on one's own feelings.

Shortly afterwards I left home to start my business career under the wing of one of my uncles who was also one of my Godparents. He encouraged me to continue church attendance. This I did, but perhaps I enjoyed driving his "straight-eight" car rather more than Matins or Evensong.

Being guided by my uncle I began to study malting and brewing and the relevant allied trades and disciplines. In hindsight those were halcyon days; I like learning and I found the industries very interesting and the people with whom I had dealings were friendly and helpful. Brewing goes on for seven days a week and it gave me scope for my energies. Then, early in 1939, I began to train in the Civil Air Guard. After landing on the first of September, the instructor told me that there would be no more C.A.G. flying for the time being, war was imminent!

Due to my excessive weight I served in the Royal Air Force not as aircrew but as an Instrument Repairer, which meant that my flying was limited to airtesting.

It was during my wartime service in the Royal Air Force that I first became involved in the occult. The instructor of a course I was attending invited a number of his students along to a demonstration of psychometry. This was something completely outside my knowledge so in my ignorance I joined in. My dictionary tells me that it means the occult power of divining properties of things by mere contact. The "psychometrist", a man in his fifties in some reserved occupation, gave messages to all my companions to which they could relate. What he said to me was totally irrelevant, I could not place any of the points that he made. This annoyed me somewhat, so I determined to persist until I met up with a "sensitive" who could tell me something of interest. To-day I realise that this was the demonic carrot that was to lead me into a very unpleasant period of my life. Gradually, slowly I wandered into the occult. Occasionally some message or situation seemed to fit into my idea of "reality", but these events were few and far between at first. As I "developed", that is sank further into the satanic situation, so the paranormal activity increased in frequency and power. Yet, during my time in the R.A.F. I attended church parades - even when they were not compulsory.

After the war I returned to civilian life, picked up the threads of my job, attended the parish church and continued in spiritism. As time went by I became increasingly perturbed over this latter activity, so I consulted my parish rector. He referred me to a senior canon in the Church of England who I assumed to be the diocesan expert. After relating the amazing things that I had witnessed during seances he assured me that I was doing very well and told me to continue! Not being completely reassured I did attend seances regularly for a further fifteen years, but I made a point of praying Our Lord's prayer before going. The uncle who had helped me so much in religious matters as well as business affairs had died during the war, but among the many happy memories one thing I remembered - he had been a Freemason.

Chapter 3

Married Life

AFTER the 1939-1945 war I met Mary, and in 1948 we married. As time went by we were blessed by the arrival of two sons. I thought that we were successful as a family. We ought to have been, with a loving wife and a couple of strapping boys growing up, but somehow, try as I might, I could not express the love that I had for them; I seemed inadequate, frustrated. We probably appeared to others to be living a normal happy life. Mary adored the children and I loved her and the two boys, but unfortunately, not as effectively as I wanted to do.

Some ten years later my wife became the leader of the church's Young Wives group and the youngsters started at the Sunday school. It was then that the Curate, a great pal, "persuaded" me to become a Sunday School teacher. This was the first occasion that I had ever had anything to do with such an establishment. Fortunately he was a very active person - he had to be, to teach me fast enough for me to keep ahead of the students in the class that he had given me. Despite all the activities I undertook, I still felt unfulfilled which, again in hindsight, was absolutely crazy. However, remembering that my uncle had been a vigorous churchman and a Freemason and had seemed content, I resolved to try to become a Mason.

I sought the advice and co-operation of a senior colleague, who was a Freemason and whose integrity I admired, on how to be made a Mason. He told me that first it was necessary for me to believe in a Supreme Being. He knew that I was a churchwarden at the time, so that that would be alright. Also he assured me that if I became a Freemason, membership of the Craft would not interfere with any of my religious beliefs.

When he explained that I needed a proposer and seconder before my name could be submitted to the Lodge for ballot, I agreed to go ahead, but only if I could be seconded by a Clerk in Holy Orders. A senior local Vicar consented and my application went forward. Some few years later he surprised me by saying that if he had his time over again he would not be made a Mason. In my admiration of the Craft and all that I thought that it stood for, this opinion seemed incredible at the time.

I had asked my earthly Father for his opinion. His comment was that he knew nothing about Freemasons nor Freemasonry, but that he would not go near them. My family and I would have been spared much sorrow if I had taken his advice.

The men whom I knew to be Masons were well respected in the community and in their own particular professions. Of the few ministers of religion that I knew at that time, both my Rector and his Curate were "on the square", that is, they were Freemasons, and I admired them very much. The Rector was one of the kindliest persons I have ever met, full of old world charm and courtesy. At one stage he had suggested that I was a suitable candidate for training in theology with the view of taking Holy Orders. This offer I declined for I had a vague idea that I did not have the requisite "anointing" - whatever that meant to me then.

My application to be admitted to a Lodge of Freemasons proved to be successful. After quite a short time I was asked to present myself at the door of the Lodge to be initiated into the Craft. Some six months later I was a Master Mason, having taken the three degrees, ceremonies, of being initiated as an Entered Apprentice, passed to the degree of a Fellowcraft and finally raised to the sublime degree of a Master Mason. These three degrees, blue masonry from the colour of the aprons, are the basic stages. One can stay at this level for one's entire masonic career if one so desires. This did not suit me, so I took the Royal Arch degree, also became a Mark Master Mason, and entered one of the so-called Christian degrees; I only attended this last degree once. Perhaps I ought to explain that the meetings of my "mother" Lodge were held monthly, the other degrees operated quarterly. As I progressed in Freemasonry I was appointed the Lodge Organist. Having played church organs for years I found the console more congenial than the workings on the floor of the Lodge. This tended to keep my mind and appraising faculties in check as I busied myself with the music.

However, as the various officers were promoted, I was made Inner Guard, the basic officer of the Lodge inside the door of the masonic temple.

As each year went by I was appointed next to Junior, then Senior Deacon, and subsequently on to Junior Warden. It was by this time I had entered the other masonic degrees, stages in advancement towards masonic truth and light.

During my first few months as Junior Warden, which I found less exacting than any previous office I began to think and reassess Freemasonry. Having been initiated some fifteen years earlier I wondered, what had I learned? what had I discovered within the Lodge that could not have been accomplished outside the Masonic Temple? Certain signs whereby I could recognise and know a fellow Freemason had been shown to me, but is this not true of the Boy Scouts? Like the other members of the Lodge I had learned much of the ritual, but where was that leading? Many of the ceremonies - the workings of the lodge - which I had witnessed had been described variously as "well done", "beautiful", "sincere" - but it was all so repetitive. Passages from the Holy Bible were quoted, but they were in contexts which were not helpful to me. Where was all this leading? As progress was made, so the prospect became increasingly pointless, perhaps with a sense of foreboding.

The "Christian Degree" that I had joined was, for me, singularly "unchristian". If this was the sort of advancement that I could expect in the so-called higher degrees then it was about time for me to take stock of my situation, seriously! As I had more time to think during my year as Junior Warden my disillusionment increased and I began

14

to consider resignation. Soon I was a member of only one Lodge, the one that had received me into Freemasonry, and in which I had spent many hours with men I admired. The Secretary was so patient with me! Somehow I knew that I must resign from all my associations with Freemasonry, but could not express my reasons adequately.

Preparing for and attending Lodge was expensive in time, and could be in money as well. Opportunities when I could have been worshipping God were spent absorbing repetitive ritual.

At last I began to realise I was not sharing the responsibility of our two sons with my wife, nor was I caring for her as she needed. These difficulties were similar for many other members as well, and if Freemasonry was truly worthwhile, why should this be? Well, I began to realise that it was not, not for me at any rate. Simply, my wife and family were too important, so I resigned from the last commitment to the Craft.

When I married Mary I was deeply involved in spiritualism without appreciating its real nature either. Also our two sons were approaching the ages for college and university. Mary and I were soon going to be able to spend more and more time together alone.

It was in the spring of 1964 that the Lord spoke to me, telling me not to go to the the intended seance on that particular evening. All that I heard was just:-

"Not tonight!".

This was the first occasion that I can remember upon which I had heard the divine voice. He sounded just as loud and as real as any human voice. All that He said was:- "Not tonight!" after I had cycled a couple of hundred yards. I returned home and rang my curate pal. He left me in no doubt at all about the extremely serious risks that I had been running. When I asked him why he had not warned me previously about these grave dangers, he responded by asking me if I would have listened to him if he had put forward the truth. Upon reflection, I don't think that I would have accepted his word before God had spoken to me. See Isaiah chapter 30: v.21.

Some six months after this incident I learned the reason why the Lord had spoken thus to me. I happened to meet in a local shop one of the members of the seance who asked me:-

"Why didn't you turn up on that evening? We were going to challenge you. Either you were to join us or we were going to throw you out."

He didn't have to explain which night he meant nor the implications. Some three years later I was completely freed from this demonic bondage. It was quite a dramatic occasion.

For some time Mary had been threatening to divorce me. She had been invited to a prayer meeting to be held in the house of a new acquaintance on a Saturday in February 1967. As she thought that it might do me some good and that it would relieve her of me for the evening she "volunteered" me and so I went. When I arrived all seats were occupied and I was invited to sit on the coal scuttle. A young man by the name of John started sharing accounts of what Jesus was doing in his experience; people being healed, it was just like a continuation of the Acts of the Apostles. No, it wasn't like the "Acts", it was acts of twentieth century followers of Jesus. This was something for which I had been searching for years and until this moment had been deluded by the counterfeit of spiritism and Freemasonry.

Very excited I returned home to relate all this to Mary. She was asleep so I went to bed. As soon as my ear touched the pillow the Lord told me that I had to see that man again. This seemed a good idea to me so I said:-

"Yes Lord."

and turned over. As my other ear touched the pillow He said again:-

"You have got to see that man again!"

Again I turned over and again He repeated:-

"You've got to see that man again"

By three o'clock in the morning two things were obvious. First the Lord was not going to allow me any sleep and secondly, I had to see this John again.

Finally I found out where he was staying and went round. When he answered the door I told him why I was there whereupon he asked for my address and then proceeded to tell me that he would call that afternoon. I couldn't dissuade him, so with misgivings I drove out to the country church where I was due to play the organ and then went home. After lunch I told Mary who was cross. She didn't want any visitors on Sunday afternoon so I was told very bluntly that I could look after them. She then told me that as soon as the two boys were off her hands, then she was going ahead with the threatened divorce proceedings. During this domestic fracas John and his wife arrived.

During the afternoon, through the ministry of John Linden-Cook and his wife, Elsa, the Lord rescued me from Satan. John and Elsa left before tea because they had to be in London in time for the 6.30 p.m. service, and it was before the construction of dual carriageways. After tea Mary told me that if I stayed as changed as I was she would not divorce me! Such was the dramatic change that the Lord had wrought in me that it was readily visible to my wife. She had changed her decision immediately.

At the time I had not realised how great was Mary's love, for the boys, yes, and also for me unworthy as I was. Some seventeen or eighteen years later Mary told me that during those dark years, the first sixteen years of our life together which ought to have been so loving, I had tried to kill her - twice. Of these events I have virtually no recollection, only the vaguest hint of one particular row that we had had in the breakfast room. Without ascertaining from her whether that was one of the occasions I cannot say for sure, but how I thank God for all of His blessings especially for His intervention at those two moments!

Towards the close of the time of ministry John had prayed that I be "baptised in the Holy Spirit" and I had received the anointing of Power from on High. This was again something new to me, I did not know what it meant or realise its significance, but the Lord so filled me with love - His Love - that it seemed as if my heart would burst if I did not share it with everyone I met. Also, the whole world seemed changed, the sky appeared bluer and grass greener, our two teenage sons were really beautiful, and my wife.....smashing! Yet this was not all, for some five years later Mary was born again of the Holy Spirit of God in the name of Jesus and similarly endowed with power from on high! This occasion I will treasure always for it seemed to me that the Lord was allowing me to see my beloved as it were through His eyes. Her beauty was such that I hardly dare touch her hand, let alone hold it, but I did and she responded by squeezing mine. Truly God was and is good!

Having received the Divine Anointing, the real nature of Freemasonry began to become apparent to me. Also, one day whilst performing one of the yoga asanas - exercises - called "Salute to the Sun", I realised that this was contrary to the Word of God. I, a child of my heavenly Father, an inheritor of the Kingdom, had been bowing down to the sun which is part of His creation. This I now realised was contrary to His explicit commands. Therefore yoga had to go. Burning all the literature that I had on the subject I repented of what I had been doing and received the Lord's forgiveness. On this occasion I actually felt a heaviness leave me.

Jesus had rescued me from Spiritualism, led me out of Freemasonry, and I had renounced and repented of all involvements with the occult so far as I knew, but there was one problem which still remained. Mary and I could not pray together when we were alone before the Lord. This difficulty stayed with us, to our mutual sorrow, for a number of years until Mary met Ione. Learning that I had been a Freemason she asked me:-

"Have you repented of and renounced Freemasonry?"

"Definitely and emphatically".

"Did you include Mary in your repentance?"

Patiently I explained that Freemasonry was an organisation involving men and men alone.

"That is where you are wrong. Your wife is affected as well. Will you re-renounce and re-repent including Mary?".

I don't think I have ever knelt down more promptly. Again I sought forgiveness for having been a Freemason and asked the Lord Jesus to completely deliver both Mary and myself from all the remaining effects. Immediately we were able to pray together for the very first time after being married for twenty-five years.

After I had been freed from Freemasonry a friend told me the true meaning of the word "Christian". Up until then I had never really bothered at all about its true significance. If I had been asked I would have said that I was a Christian. Of course I was a Christian, born in England of Christian parents, christened as a baby, then confirmed and thereafter I went reasonably regularly to church - Church of England. In addition there was the joy of driving out to country churches on roads that were almost free of traffic. To my sorrow and shame I thought little or nothing about the members of other denominations, what ideas I did have were just hearsay, uninformed and probably uncharitable.

During my time of service in the R.A.F. I managed to pass muster on the piano or whatever on church parades when required to play. People used to look up to me, they expected my behaviour to be exemplary. I remember that after one tiny slip of the tongue I was told that they didn't expect such behaviour from me! Yes, I was a "Christian" - and a prig!

Jesus was faithful and He still is. He had kept me and He had now rescued me from all my associations with Satan and his demons in the occult, the enticing, secret broad pathways to hell, secret only as regards their destination. Although I had continued to attend church services they were unsatisfying and somehow becoming banal, pointless. I had observed Sunday as a day apart as far as my job allowed. It was a day of rest which I interpreted broadly speaking as doing what I wanted to do and not doing anything I didn't want to do - if I could get out of it. But now my life had been completely changed and then this friend, Freddie, defined "Christian" for me - "A Little Anointed One".

This was a revelation to me. I meditated long over it. If Jesus of Nazereth was the Christ of God, that is, His Anointed One, - Greek Christos - then, of course the diminutive, "Christian" - Greek "christianos" - means a little anointed one. This is simple so far. What was this "anointing"? It was nothing less than the descending of God the Holy Spirit in power upon Jesus, the Son of God. This was a spiritual blessing, so how could it apply to me?

Light began to dawn upon me. Jesus had been born of the Holy Spirit. We are told of His birth, escape into Egypt, and His coming of age ceremony when He was twelve years old, but nothing else until He met with His cousin John the Baptist in the river Jordan. At the descent of the dove of the Holy Spirit, Jesus of Nazareth became Jesus the Christ, the Anointed of God.

Hadn't Jesus told Nicodemus, recorded by John in chapter 3 verse 3, that unless he was born again of the Spirit of God he could not even see the Kingdom of God?

(Jesus bestowed this miracle of new birth on the disciples when they were together in the upper room on the day of His resurrection.)

Then Luke, at the close of his account of the Gospel and at the beginning of his record of the Acts of the Apostles, speaks of receiving power from on high when the Holy Spirit has come upon you. This was beginning to make sense, yes, it all added up. I did believe that Jesus was the Son of God, had come on earth as a man, had died for my sins and had been brought back to life by the power of God's Holy Spirit. He had ascended back to heaven to His Father, and now mine. I knew that I had been clothed with the same power of the Holy Spirit!

Chapter 4

Out of Freemasonry

THIS release from demonic bondage, this new appreciation of joy, real JOY kept bubbling up - and spilling over! At two o'clock in the afternoon I had been under the sentence of impending divorce; a couple of hours later Mary had removed the threat. It took quite a time for me to come to terms with the dramatic change in my circumstances. The love I had for Mary reached depths, or is it heights? that previously I had not known existed. Having confessed all as best I could to Our Father in the Name of Jesus, He had forgiven me and so too had dear Mary! Our life together blossomed out miraculously, each day was happier than the day before, but what of our two sons? Until I had been delivered from these forces of evil our life together had been hellish. The youngsters had been able to get away from me to have some relief at school, but poor Mary had been lumbered with me more or less full time. Now Mary and I were freed after sixteen years. Then God told me what I had to do for our sons. To prevent the sins of their father being visited upon them I had to give them back to our heavenly Father - publicly. This was not easy, but it was so poignant to tell them what I had done and to explain the reasons to them personally. It had to be done - anything to prevent what I had done and been through from having any effect upon them or upon anybody else.

One other memory from this period returns to me. I had been invited to go on a diocesan retreat, my first. It was led by the Bishop. I remember button-holing him in my exuberance for half-an-hour to tell him what Jesus had done for me and my family. It was all so new, so exciting that I had to share the news with everyone!

Days, weeks went by and the memory of my occult activities faded rapidly for both of us now that we were growing in God's Love and in love towards each other. Being filled with the Love of God enabled me to love Him, Mary, our family, anyone. At the actual moment of receiving the anointing of the Holy Spirit I felt as if I should burst. When I shared this experience with my especial clerical friend he took great heart and promptly told me I ought to become a Lay Reader in the Church of England. True to his word I received my provisional licence a couple of days later. I thoroughly enjoyed the training course and later to be admitted and licensed as a Reader. Surely it is one of the greatest privileges to share the grace of Jesus with another soul, to see them respond and to be born again of the Holy Spirit of God.

Shortly after I had severed all connections with Freemasonry my company was in the market for a moderately expensive machine. A senior member of one of the interested manufacturers made it blatantly obvious that he was a Freemason hoping, presumably, that I would respond and do what I could so that his company would be awarded the contract. Perhaps a mutual acquaintance had told him that I was a Mason for he persisted in giving the signs by which Freemasons can recognise one another. I felt nauseated that business could be approached in such a way. In fairness I feel certain that there are many who range under the banner of Freemasonry to-day who would agree with me in my disgust. My other feeling was that of relief, for I could not, indeed must not now acknowledge the signs for I was now no longer a Freemason. Thankfully the decision did not rest with me though his machine was selected.

Although nothing to do with the burden of this book, it was the only machine I have ever met that needed a major overhaul before it was commissioned - which increased my sense of relief at the timing of my freedom. This was purely a business encounter with possible moral overtones, but it served to emphasise to me the nature of the Brotherhood.

As time went by I became increasingly aware that Freemasonry was not of God, the Father of my Lord and Saviour Jesus Christ. I began to realise the demonic content of the rituals and ceremonies I had witnessed and in which I had participated. In none of the degrees I had taken had Jesus been proclaimed as Lord despite a number of texts taken from the Bible. Thus, if Jesus was not the Lord of Freemasonry, then there was only one other candidate, Satan, and he had had the effrontery to quote from the Scriptures to Jesus Himself, for example, during the time of His temptations - Matthew 4: 6.

If the worship of Satan as Master was the "summum bonum", the ultimate objective of the Craft, then, if I may be permitted one "Hallelujah", I was truly glad to be out of it all. But what about the Brethren whom I had come to know and respect who were left behind? What could I do? What should I do? Almost without exception, every time I have made an approach to a Brother I have been repulsed, often as a pariah.

When God leads, however, the response is totally different! A wife and her elderly mother arrived at our farm one morning for a chat and coffee. Mary and I were both at home for I was on holiday. Shortly before they left the wife shared her concern for her husband. I knew that he had been a Freemason and had thought that he had resigned from his Lodge. This she confirmed, but he was suffering bouts of black depression. They had been going on for about nine months and were getting worse. In answer to my queries she agreed that he had resigned from his Lodge but that he had not disposed of all his regalia. Bearing in mind that I had burned all the masonic books and certificates that I had had, and also the Lord had told me to return all monies paid to me for all my regalia, aprons and sashes etc. back to the purchaser, I advised the lady to tell her husband to burn the lot leaving nothing, absolutely nothing.

Mary and I were finishing lunch when the husband rang up asking if he could come over to see us. He duly arrived with an armful of masonic material. I shared with him that I was convinced that Freemasonry was demonic at source and that

26

he ought to be completely cleansed - delivered - from this satanic influence over his life, and that he should burn all that he had brought, for he had assured me that he had brought all that he possessed in this connection with him.

He agreed readily, and we knelt down on the hearth. I explained that the Greek of the last petition of Our Lord's Prayer could be rendered:-

"Deliver us from the evil one"

Would he agree to pray this whole prayer with me and to have faith that, as it is the prayer that Jesus Himself taught, He would honour our faith and all evil spirits would be cleaned out?

"Yes, I will"!

After praying this prayer together we thanked the Lord for this deliverance. Then I gave him a box of matches and told him to be my guest and use the old farmhouse fireplace. Surprisingly quickly the flames reduced even the books to ashes. It was about three o'clock when this ex-Mason left to return to his office. Imagine the joy when he telephoned a couple of hours later. He sounded so happy; all the depressions had gone, he KNEW that they had gone. The backache which had been incapacitating him for some six months had also gone!

Replacing the telephone receiver I thought of the woman who had been bound by Satan for eighteen years (Luke 12: 16.) Jesus is still the same today!

Chapter 5

Early Christian Life

HAVING been freed from demonic domination I would like to share some of the occasions in which the Lord has been blessing us. God's way of dealing with us, His children, is His prerogative. Sometimes it is so simple that even I can see what is happening; at other times He leads us step by step to test and strengthen our faith. As an example of the latter, in March three years ago Mary was called into hospital to undergo surgery. Part of me objected to this very strenuously, yet the fact was all too clear, she had not been healed by divine authority in the Name of Jesus. Equally it was apparent that something had to be done and done promptly. Mary, an S.R.N. when we married, was quite resigned and reasonably happy to go in. On the afternoon of the operation the telephone rang. It was Mary as cheerful as ever:-

"You can come and pick me up"!

Driving home she told me that she had been given all the due premedications and had been taken down to the operating theatre when a messenger from the "path lab" reported to the surgeon that the operation must not take place because this patient was too anaemic!

After six months of iron treatment Mary went

back into another hospital. This time I was curiously relaxed and acquiescent. On the evening of the operating day I rang up and was assured that all had gone well. I went to bed very early, around eight o'clock. As soon as I lay down I had to pray for Mary. I could not explain this, I had no thoughts in my mind except that I was to pray for her, lying flat on my back on the bed. Nothing like this had ever happened to me before, yet with all this burden of prayer I felt beautifully at peace - "the peace of the Lord that passes all understanding". Some two or maybe even three hours later the load was lifted and I promptly turned over and peacefully went to sleep.

When I saw Mary on the following day, yes, she was sore but reasonably perky. I told her of my prayer experience of the previous evening, we thought little more about it at the time. Some days later on the way home after she had been released from the hospital, Mary shared a few more details. At the time that I had been praying, interceding for her, Mary had haemorrhaged very badly, and the key to the blood bank could not be found! The other patients in the ward had told her a day or so before she was discharged. She had refrained from telling me in case I blew up at the medical staff. Praise God, our faith, Mary's and mine was greatly strengthened by this incident when Jesus demonstrated His sovereign power in His sovereign way.

After a couple of days at home it became apparent that something was not quite right. A quick visit to our local doctor and Mary was on her way back to hospital without waiting for an ambulance or even going back home to collect the requisite necessities for such an occasion. Amazingly we were not perturbed. I did not understand what the Lord was doing, but I knew His hand was upon Mary and upon me. Whilst I was waiting in the corridor outside the ward for some news from the nursing staff He spoke to me:-

"Trust Me"!

A few minutes later He spoke again:-

"I know what I am doing"!

What an encouragement, how edifying to my faith were His words, for I hadn't the faintest idea what was happening - or why.

Visiting Mary on the following morning she was still in pain, but the hospital staff assured us both that all was well, but that they would like to keep her in for a day or two "to make sure", then she could come home. In the next two hours we found out that the Lord was going to make sure also!

My way home for the first few miles was straight along a main road. Suddenly, after a couple of hundred yards the car turned left into another main road and then almost immediately turned right, across the traffic and into a side road - without hitting anything of course. Once into this side road I felt free to drive the car under my own guidance. Turning the first corner, directly facing me was a large notice board outside a place of worship. Along the bottom was quoted Proverbs 3: 5,6:-

"Trust in the Lord with all your heart and do not lean on your own understanding.

In all your ways acknowledge Him and He will make your paths straight."

Four days later when I took Mary and her sister, who was staying with us to help with the "invalid", round that way to show them, the whole board had been taken down.

What was it that the Lord desired to ensure? Over a solitary lunch at the farm I was convinced that He wanted me to be baptised - the believer's baptism by full immersion. On the return journey to the hospital that afternoon to see Mary I decided that, in view of her condition, suggestions on this subject would not be too tactful. However, when I opened my mouth to greet her, out it came. Then Mary amazed me when she responded that she had been discussing the same topic over lunch with the lady in the next bed but one.

It almost goes without saying that as soon as Mary was sufficiently recovered and was able to be immersed we were both baptised as an act of obedience. This was not all; we were examined to see if we knew what we were doing, did we mean business? Would we share our testimonies? Whilst describing my confirmation as a lovely occasion, the sun shining through curved roseate windows, the tints of red and gold in the recess behind the holy table.....I suddenly realised that this was an entirely spiritual conception for the church in which I was confirmed had no curves, no stained glass and it was raining at the time.

Although I had wandered far into forbidden territory Jesus had remained faithful to His commitment to me, for I had meant business when I was confirmed at sixteen years of age.

Now that Mary and I had obeyed and had been baptised in water as well as in the Holy Spirit, the Lord had work for us to do.

Shortly afterwards we were invited to an F.G.B.M.F.I. dinner in a neighbouring town. After a very pleasant evening, as we were preparing to leave, someone pointed out another man on the other side of the room who had a very exciting testimony. As I think all testimonies are thrilling, the hand of Almighty God in action, I made my way over to him; it was too good an opportunity to miss. He was on the point of leaving when I reached him so, after an exchange of courtesies, I gave him my card.

Some weeks later he telephoned inviting us both over for high tea. Agreeably surprised we accepted and the four of us spent a pleasant time together wandering round their lovely bungalow and garden. During the meal, however, I realised that our host, even if he wasn't a Freemason, knew too much about the Craft for the benefit of his health. Not thinking for a moment what his reaction might be I asked him:-

"What do you know about Freemasonry?"

"I am a Freemason, and I am up to the twenty-fifth degree".

"Then you've got problems!"

Praise God, he wanted to know more. Was I a Freemason? Had I been one? Why should I speak like this about such an honourable institution?

God had gone before us for our host told us that he had been having second thoughts about the

Brotherhood, whether to continue his membership. It took only a couple of illustrations from the ritual to convince him that it was not of God. Then he asked me what he should do.

My advice was that he should repent of his involvement in the occult and renounce Freemasonry on behalf of his wife and himself. They both knelt on the dining room carpet while he confessed his sin to God the Father in the name of Jesus and asked for forgiveness and release for his wife and for himself. Then I suggested that he burned all his masonic regalia, books and certificates. He left the room to collect his equipment, but seemed to have some doubts on his return. These were soon resolved, his house had central heating and therefore no fireplaces, so we had a bonfire in the garden.

As it was blazing away he remarked that he knew how it was that I had recognised him as a Freemason. I replied that that might be so, but it did not alter the fact that whilst he had been out of the room Mary had said to me that the Lord had told her before we had left our home that we were going out on a "Freemasonry" trip. She would not have allowed me to leave his house without first challenging him. This amazed him, but he soon realised that the loving hand of God had been stretched out in his direction to rescue both him and his wife.

It is such a thrill to be on the Lord's business together with Mary especially when He speaks to us individually for she had not mentioned His Word until our host had left us in the dining room with his wife.

Chapter 6

A Christian Glance at Freemasonry

I WOULD like to consider the implications of Freemasonry from the position of a redeemed child of God and endowed with His divine authority.

Can Freemasonry be considered an institution that is a superior sort of benevolent society, a select club for worthy men, a brotherhood that provides for professional men a haven and escape from the rat race of the world?

There is the Masonic Hospital with Royal favour that is reputed to be one of the finest in the United Kingdom, if not in the whole world. Then there is "The Grand Charity" to give help towards elderly masons. Finally there are the two excellent schools for boys and for girls, the children of indigent Freemasons. Bearing all this in mind and also the generous donations to non-masonic causes, the Royal National Lifeboat Institution for one example, it is easy to think that Freemasonry cannot be all that bad. Unfortunately it is!

Putting on one side all the secrets of Freemasonry, the signs of recognition, let us look briefly at some of the spoken words. As we do, let us remember the words of Jesus when He said that it is what proceeds out of the mouth, that defiles the man. See for example Matthew 15: 11.

At his initiation the Candidate is introduced by the Tyler to the Inner Guard and thence to the Worshipful Master of the Lodge as being "poor and in a state of darkness". This was sprung upon me without warning, and being blindfolded at the time did not help me to think. The Tyler, armed with a drawn sword, stands on guard outside a locked door, the entrance to the Lodge.

Consider what he is saying from a spiritual aspect, for this is the only way in which to appraise anything in Freemasonry. The chief qualification demanded of me before my name went forward to the ballot by members of the Lodge was that I believed in a Supreme Spiritual Being. In my mind that title belonged only to God the Father of Jesus of Nazareth, but I suppose it could be applied to the heads of any other religion or faith. Could it be ascribed to Satan? He sees himself as the Prince of this world, the power of the air, the avowed enemy of God vying for the position of supreme authority over the whole universe. Jesus refers to a ruler and prince of this world in terms that identify Satan in this role. See, for example, Matthew chapter 4. v.9 where Jesus does not contradict Satan.

As I am now a child of God and an inheritor of the Kingdom of Heaven, having eternal life and being clothed with power from on high, how could I be described as being poor? My heavenly Father of His own good pleasure, through Jesus, had given me His Kingdom. No way can I be considered poor when the Father has lavished His love upon me in such a manner. As for being in a state of darkness the hoodwink ensured that from the natural point of view, but the whole issue is in the supernatural, spiritual realm. If it were not so I wonder if Freemasonry would ever have developed as it has. To deny that there is light, spiritual light in the world is blasphemy, putting at nought in one sentence the entire burden of the Bible. See for example Genesis 1: 3:-

"Then God said, "Let there be light"; and there was light."

and that means His light, not the light of the sun, moon and stars for they were not created until the fourth day - vv. 14-19.

Here at the very outset of one's Masonic career it is implied quite clearly that outside the door of the Lodge is spiritual darkness; spiritual light, salvation is to be found inside the Lodge, in the Craft. This may sound too strong a statement, but is it? If Satan always spoke the truth, the whole truth and nothing but the truth would his counterfeit domain attract the attention of any sane person? Who would want to be made a Freemason if he were told that he was entering black bondage?

Much is spoken of the benefit of "Masonic Light" during the rehearsals of the rituals, yet the Candidate is hoodwinked, that is blindfolded, before his entry into the first degree on his Initiation, and upon his exaltation into the degree of the "Holy Royal Arch". In the third degree, that of raising, much of the ceremony takes place when the temple is illuminated by one dim lamp. All masonic working, so far as I know, takes place behind a closed door, locked and doubly guarded. The Tyler stands outside with his drawn sword.

The Inner Guard, armed with a poniard, locks and secures the entrance from the inside, opening the door only in response to the correct code of knocks.

What a contrast this all is to Jesus in John 8: 12 and 36:-

"Again therefore Jesus spoke to them saying, 'I am the light of the world; he who follows Me shall not walk in darkness, but shall have the light of life'".

"If therefore the Son shall make you free, you shall be free indeed".

In his account of the Gospel Luke records in chapter 12: 2,3:-

"But there is nothing covered up that will not be revealed, and hidden that will not be known". "Accordingly whatever you have said in the dark shall be heard in the light, and what you have whispered in the inner rooms shall be proclaimed from the housetops".

all words from the mouth of Jesus Himself.

So we must face up to the purpose of Freemasonry. At one and the same time I held a number of lay appointments in the Church of England and also various offices in Freemasonry. For years I did not see any incompatibility between the two callings, but thought rather that they were complementary. If they were not on the same line, at least they were on parallel lines.

The introduction by the Tyler at my initiation served to heighten the mystery of the secret aspect of the Craft. Youngsters of all ages are often intrigued when confronted by the situation wherein "somebody knows something that you don't know". Isn't this a lovely carrot - "Masonry is a peculiar system of morality, veiled in allegory and illustrated by symbols"? I swallowed it all for some 15 years.

The Initiate is also informed that:-

"No other institution can boast of a firmer foundation than that of Freemasonry".

How can a Christian accept this? It is an amazing fact that the implications of this had escaped me completely until I became free, a Freed-mason. Satan had me very closely blinkered, for this means that the Masonic Arts are equal, at least, to the Bible in authority and truth. We must continue to remember that we are considering this situation on the spiritual level. Who would dare to presume to equality with the Word of God?

Luke records for us in the Acts of the Apostles, the activities of the young church, in chapter 4 from vv. 8 to 12:-

"Then Peter, filled with the Holy Spirit said to them...let it be known to all of you.....that by the Name of Jesus the Nazarene....by this Name this man stands before you in good health....and there is salvation in no one else; for there is no other Name under heaven that has been given among men, by which we must be saved".

This dichotomy is also clear from verse 11:-

"He is the stone which was rejected by you, the builders, but which became the very corner stone".

All superb and stately edifices have their foundation stones. To-day they are affixed in a prominent position and record items of general interest, when unveiled and by whom etc. At the time of Jesus' earthly ministry they had a much more practical use. The stone was sited at one corner of the proposed building and the main walls took their positions and directions therefrom. How can THE corner stone, Jesus, as proclaimed by Peter be compared with the statement of the Worshipful Master of the Lodge who assures the Candidate that:-

"he has been placed in the north-east corner of the lodge emblematically to represent such a stone"

and is adjured:-

"to erect on the stone laid this evening an edifice perfect in all its parts"?

Yet at my initiation I found it was quite a stimulating thought, to be encouraged to do something for myself, to be helped by the aid of the masonic arts to make my life worthwhile. When I first heard this exhortation, addressed to me, I was thrilled. After much that I had not comprehended, after parts of the ceremony that were not really to my liking, this, I thought, was the beginning of the meat of Freemasonry.

Earlier in the ceremony of my initiation, after the perambulations around the temple, I had been told to kneel in a specific position. A voice which I had assumed to be that of the Worshipful Master demanded of me:-

"What in your present position is the predominant desire of your heart?"

Before I could say what I was thinking a very prompt prompt from my guide, the Junior Deacon as I was later to discover, came:-

"Light".

As the Worshipful Master instructed:-

"Let that blessing be restored to the Candidate".

The hoodwink was removed adroitly and I found myself looking straight at the Volume of the Sacred Law, the Holy Bible, lying open on a pedestal before me.

Although I was assured that it was one of the great lights in Freemasonry, nothing was ever read out of the Bible that evening, nor during all the years I spent in the Craft. This is puzzling; how can any book, however emblematical, shed any light on proceedings if it is not read and studied?

This and other critical thoughts were overshadowed by such ideas as erecting a stately edifice, something that I could and would do, something I was going to be shown, progress that I was about to make that I failed to discern what I now think is the real truth about Freemasonry, what I am now certain is the reality behind the Craft, Satan. As I did not become aware of this for many years, then the brainwashing was effective in my case. It was so good that I can remember only two discordant notes ever being sounded. Once I was asked to play more lively music in Lodge and once I was informed that the translation in the ritual of one or two of the Hebrew words used in the Royal Arch degree were not correct. Before we pursue these thoughts further I will turn to others and relate some of their experiences.

Chapter 7

The Testimony of Ron Price

IT was on the recommendation of the Treasurer to the Church Council that I joined Freemasonry in 1960. He suggested that as I was on very close terms with him and a good churchman, I might consider joining. I knew about Freemasonry because my father was a past master; my oldest brother was, and still is, a Grand Lodge Officer although he does not practise now. So when I was approached, this is what I told him. He replied that there would be:- "no problem over your acceptance; you're what is known as a 'Lewis', so you're O.K.!" (A Lewis is a son of a Freemason - Ed.).

My name went forward and in due course I was told to get ready for initiation, have a dark suit, a black tie and a white shirt; I just turned up! I never asked any questions as to what it was all about and no information was offered; but I thought, well, Dad's been in it. I remember him getting up in his regalia at home as clear as anything - I was about eleven or twelve years old at the time - and I can remember him with a little book memorising things. I didn't know what he was doing but that is what it looked like. It was never discussed. We were a Christian home, or what appeared to be a Christian home, we went to church, so I had no qualms about joining the Freemasons. I went along and there I was!

When I got there I was prepared as an Entered Apprentice. I didn't know it was an entered apprentice ceremony, but I was just prepared, divested of all money and metal and "roll your sleeves up, open your shirt" and I thought:-

"Oh Lord, this seems a bit queer!"

but it never crossed my mind to question it at all. I don't know why I didn't. Then this blindfold was put on, I was led in, I took the oaths and all the rest - I never questioned it at all. I couldn't anyway, that's how deep my knowledge of the Bible was. So I became a Freemason and continued for eight years.

Then I got on to the Lodge of Instruction, once a month during the lodge season of six months. It was not a Lodge of Instruction, rather a Lodge of Rehearsal, that was all. You had one of the four instructors who were responsible for the Lodge of Instruction and he would tell you how you had done the various things. (Recited that particular portion of the ritual - Ed.) I was presented with my book of rituals, memorised it and went along for the first time where various people were taking the different parts. So then we were asked to volunteer for the next time. I had been through all three degrees to that of a Master Mason before I went to the Lodge of Instruction. During this period I re-hearsed every part, every officership including the Worshipful Master, the whole lot.

In the Lodge of Instruction we did not do the Junior Warden's "Charge to the Initiate", we just rehearsed the Junior Warden's part up to the end of the initiation, to the end of each ceremony in fact, but not this particular "Charge". So I never learned it.

I then got on to the list of stewards and worked my way up, waiting at the tables with the wine. (This at the banquet after all Masonic business in the Temple had been completed - Ed.) At the table you had the various speeches, but one thing did concern me, there was a desire among the speakers always to tell a certain kind of joke. Their humour was not the sort that I really appreciated.

Then came January 1976 and I was appointed or elected, I'm not sure which, to the office of Junior Warden, having gone through the duties of Inner Guard, Junior and Senior Deacons. I had done those jobs perfectly and so I became Junior Warden. In February 1976 we had an initiation ceremony, so I had to learn the Junior Warden's Charge. Well; I started to learn it and as I did .... one of the opening clauses is:-

"No other institution can boast a more solid foundation than that on which Freemasonry rests".

and as I said this, the Holy Spirit, as I now recognise Him, said to me:-

"You cannot say that!"

I had been born again in October 1974, and I had been filled with the Spirit as well, so I had been a Christian for only fourteen months up to that point. I had attended Lodge as Junior and Senior Deacons and I had heard this "Charge" but had not been concerned about it; it had just gone in and out. My wife had become a Christian on New Year's Day 1976, It was in February 1976, as Junior Warden, that I had to do this "Charge" and as I started.....

"You cannot say this, you have accepted Me as Lord, you cannot say that another institution has a firmer foundation than Me!"

"You are right, God!"

Anyway, I did the ceremony in February and blow me, March, another initiation, again I had to go through this. Again the Spirit said:-

"You cannot keep saying this, there is only one thing, you have got to resign!"

I didn't know quite what to do.

I had started going to Birmingham Cathedral for a businessmen's service at which a few women were present. David McInnes gave the address; just half-an-hour with a hymn and address and that was it. On one Tuesday I said to David:-

"I am in the Freemasons".

and I explained to him how the Lord had told me to resign. He said:-

"You can't just send a letter of resignation saying to the Worshipful Master "I am resigning", you can't stay away, you have got to be a witness! So you must write a letter and state clearly the Christian principle on which you are resigning".

So I wrote to the Worshipful Master. Now even the term "worshipful master" sticks in my gullet, and right from that time it has. I also wrote to the Lodge secretary.

In Lodge you are not to talk about your Christian faith. As I had become a "born again" Christian I had talked with the secretary about the way in which my life was changing and my views were changing. So when he received my letter of resignation, he rang up and said:-

"Thank you for your letter, I am very sorry indeed to see this, but in view of the conversations you have had with me recently I can fully understand it".

Then I had a 'phone call from the Worshipful Master:-

"We are in the middle of a lodge year and I would like us to meet to discuss this matter".

"O.K. where would you like to meet?"

So we met at a local pub. We sat out in the garden with a drink and we started talking:-

"You can see, I just cannot carry on, I've become a committed Christian, accepted Jesus as my Lord and I cannot say that any institution has a more solid foundation".

I have a little "Gideon" testament in my pocket. I pulled it out:-

"That's my Bible, that's what I believe. I believe that it is the inspired Word of God. Do you believe it?"

"No. That is two thousand years ago!"

"No! it is for to-day".

"My father is a Methodist Lay Minister and I am on the board that selects Methodist Ministers. I do not find anything incompatible".

"Well, that is up to you, but I cannot accept it".

"You are putting me on the spot a bit, right in the middle of the year and I must share with you part of the meetings we held before I was made

Master. As Master-Elect it was discussed whom I would have as my Wardens, I said that I wanted you as J.W. There was one person who wasn't very happy with you being appointed but as Master-Elect I over-ruled him. What am I going to say to him now?"

"That's up to you, that is your problem, not mine. I must be obedient to what my Lord has told me".

"You took an oath on it!"

"Yes, but I should not have ever taken an oath, that was contrary to the Word. The promise I have given to Jesus is far greater than the oath I have taken in Lodge. I have got to be obedient to that one!"

We agreed to part. I was not going to withdraw my resignation and go on to the end of the year. No! I just couldn't carry on, my conscience would not let me. So that was it and out I came.

When I came out of Freemasonry I was concerned about my regalia, books, etc. and I thought I would take them down to the Lodge and give them all to the Tyler for some future candidate, it might save him some money. Again the Holy Spirit spoke to me:-

"You can't do that!"

"Why not Lord?"

"You do that and you are going to encourage someone into something that you know is not part of Me."

"So what do you want me to do with it, Lord?"

"Take it up the garden and burn it."

So up the garden path I went. I have an incinera

tor up there, I took the case, two aprons - by that time I had entered the Royal Arch. I burned the R.A. apron and sash, master mason apron and books and tried to forget it all. As it burned I felt a load come off me and I felt free!

Shortly after that I went round to the lady who had laid hands on me in October 1974 when I was born again and filled with the Spirit and told her what I had done. She said:-

"Praise the Lord! Neither Joan nor I knew that you were a Freemason but we prayed that if you were you would come out of it."

What the Lord had revealed to me very simply since my resignation was that Masonry is a counterfeit church; the Trinity as was revealed to me was the Master and the two Wardens, in the Royal Arch it is Zerubbabel, Haggai and Joshua (The titles of the three principle officers of the Royal Arch degree - Ed.) They are basically the Trinity in each case. The Lodge room is described as a temple; there are hymns and prayers which never mention Jesus. I never received any personal instruction that I must not talk about Jesus but I think it was implicit that politics and religion were not mentioned. Therefore this was a new thing to see that this was another church. What confirmed this to me was that one Past Master, who was a member of the congregation of the church when I first joined it, had declared at one point that he didn't get as much out of coming to Church as he got out of going to the Lodge. That has always stuck with me for we had a tremendous preacher in that Church.

Chapter 8

The Testimony of John Walker

I THINK that God is calling His people to-day to be obedient and I say this really out of regret. For one thing, I was heavily involved in Freemasonry, in three orders. I now know that it is of the Enemy, it is Satanic, it is not of God! It is a way of ensnaring men into something that is of the occult. I say quite categorically to any Christian man in Freemasonry, I must say to you, in love, you must come out because you cannot serve two Masters. I was involved, as I say, in three orders, in Craft Masonry, Royal Arch, and Knights Templar.

Just to illustrate some of the things you have to do in the Holy Royal Arch, one has to bow down to a block of stone. Carved on that block are the names of Jehovah, Jah, Bul and On. Jah is an abbreviation of Jehovah of the Bible and the God Whom we adore. Bul is an abbreviation of Baal, and On is an abbreviation of the Egyptian god Osiris. What a travesty that a Christian should go into a lodge and bow down to a block of stone with that on.

Now in God's Word Jesus says:-

"I am the Way, the Truth and the Life, no one comes to the Father but by Me."

so how can a Christian, a born again believer, bow down to a block of stone with these names on it?

There are many other things; Masonry teaches salvation by good works. I now know that salvation is a free gift of grace. Freemasons talk in terms of the Volume of the Sacred Law, which is open in any Freemason's Lodge. In this country (England - Ed.) it can be the Bible, but it could be just as easily the Book of Mormon, the Koran, the Vedas or any other of the so-called Scriptures of the world - and there are 27 of them - that is used in the Lodge as the Volume of the Sacred Law.

Everything about the Freemason's ceremony, the ritual, in many ways imitates the things that are totally anti-church, anti-Christ. There are three principle officers in a Craft Lodge: the Worshipful Master, Senior and Junior Wardens. All of these, in many ways, represent God the Father, God the Son (Jesus) and God the Holy Spirit. Everything is a sort of perversity of Christianity - and I was engrossed in it! I enjoyed the friendship, I enjoyed the people that I met and, I suppose if I am truly honest, that I enjoyed the work contacts that it gave me.

After coming into the baptism of the Holy Spirit, every single time I went to a Lodge meeting I would have distinct unease about it. I didn't mind the dinners afterwards, but with the actual ritual and ceremony I felt a total unease.

Then quite an extraordinary thing happened because I had to go to Gloucester for a consecration of a Knights Templar Preceptory, a very rare event. I went along and arrived something over an hour early. At that particular consecration, believe it or not, there was a Bishop and five other clergy of the

49

Anglican church present. It just shows you the hold Freemasonry has over the upper echelons of the Establishment in this land.

But I was early, so I went for a walk round the town. Just across the way from where the Masonic Temple was there was a Christian bookshop and right in the middle of the window at that particular time was a display. There was a purple band across the middle of the book which read:-

"Can a Christian be a Freemason?"

That hit me like a sledgehammer. I had never really thought about it up to that time. Now, every single time I went into a bookshop - just as if God wanted to show me something - I would pull out a book and it would be all about Christianity and Freemasonry and why a Christian should not, could not be a Freemason. I was so angry that I would slam the book back on the shelf. I said:-

"Lord, what is the matter with Freemasonry? I am enjoying it, I want to carry on, I want to be involved."

But at that time I started to pray very earnestly:-

"Lord, if You want me to come out of Freemasonry, I'll come out, but You've got to do something dramatic to get me out. I am not going to come out just because of these books. I believe that if You want me to come out You will do something tremendously dramatic."

At this time I was the secretary of my own professional institution, the West Midlands Surveyors' division. On a Monday evening we had our normal committee meeting. I came out of that meeting and got into my car. I drive regularly, and

I leave the radio switched on so that when you turn the ignition on, it comes on as well straight away. I drove down the road and who should jump out but my old boss. I stopped the car, wound down the window and we had a fairly lengthy chat. We exchanged pleasantries, he asked me how the work situation was going and I wished him "Goodnight."

I started the car again, but this time, although the engine started first time, there was no radio. It was completely and utterly dead. All the way home I was switching the radio "on" and "off", pressing button after button in, nothing happened at all.

I got to within a mile of my home just outside Sutton Coldfield on the north side of Birmingham, when suddenly a voice as audible as I am speaking to you now said:-

"Ask anything in My Name and it will be given unto you. Command this radio to come on."

I thought I was going out of my mind, I really thought I was hearing voices and so I did nothing. Yet that same Voice came back again:-

"Ask anything in My Name and it will be given unto you. Command this radio to come on."

And so I did.

Do you know, nothing happened. So I said:-

"Lord, I'm sorry, I'm just hearing things."

The Voice came back again:-

"Good, you have obeyed Me. Now leave this radio on in the switched "on" position because when you stop this car and start it again, this radio will come on."

I drove to my home. Normally my wife would leave the "up and over" garage door up so that I could just turn in off the road, straight into the garage, get out of the car and go into the house. On this particular evening she had left the door down, so I left the car in the road, got out, lifted the garage door, got back into the car and immediately the radio came on! I was so amazed. I rushed into the house and told my wife and family exactly what had happened. Then I rang Chris in my office and asked him:-

"Chris, do you really think these sort of things really happen?"

And he said:-

"John, of course they happen. I believe that was a test of obedience. The Lord will call upon you to honour that in a much greater way."

Little did I know the significance of that because in fact on the Saturday morning of that same week, we had an F.G.B.M.F.I. chapter breakfast. I spoke to the president of the our chapter and told him the story just as I have told you. He said:-

"John, I think that is quite exciting. I think you ought to share it with the people in the room sometime during the breakfast."

So I did just that, I shared just exactly as I have shared with you now and concluded by saying that I am just waiting to find out what that test of obedience is.

Our speaker that morning was Ron Price, who had stepped in at the last minute. It was the very first time that Ron had spoken at a meeting.

Suddenly, halfway through, he said:-

"I believe there are Freemasons in this room."

He went on to share why you could not be a Freemason. You can imagine the sense of conviction which was in my heart at that particular time. I knew that this was the test of obedience that I was called upon to honour. There and then I renounced Freemasonry, I went straight home and within an hour I had renounced all my connections with Freemasonry; no one could understand it. The Lord never makes it easy for us does He?

That particular evening I had to go to have dinner with two members of the Lodge. The first thing that I said was that I had renounced Freemasonry. They looked absolutely askance at me.

We had dinner and afterwards they said:-

"John, you have got to tell us why you have done this."

So for two hours Margaret and I shared Jesus with them, what He had done and why I felt led to take the action I had taken. Praise God, three weeks later one of those men 'phoned me up to tell me that he had decided to get confirmed in the Anglican church and his wife had also completely rededicated her life; in fact we went along to their Confirmation.

On the Wednesday of the following week I had to have a business lunch with an architect. We were a young firm and we rely heavily on architects to give us work - and he was the Worshipful Master of a Lodge. I met him for lunch; the first thing I said to him was:-

"Gwyn, the first thing you have got to know is that I have renounced Freemasonry because Jesus

Christ is more important to me than Freemasonry. I cannot belong to it any longer."

I'll never forget the look he gave me. He said:-

"JOHN YOU ARE A FOOL!"

And I thought, my goodness, there is all that work gone completely out of the window. But God's Word says that:-

"My God will supply all my needs according to His riches in glory by Christ Jesus."

That architect now gives us at least five times as much work now as he did then. There is not a time when we are not working for him. I have not influenced him in any shape or form except that occasionally he will call me into his office and say:-

"Sit down, give me a few more details, you might convert me."

I have often spoken to him for an hour at a time; isn't this wonderful? Praise the Lord!

Chapter 9

The Testimony of
James Hickman

I WAS a Freemason. As an initiate I was told that I was in a state of darkness. Because I had been blindfolded I related this to a physical darkness at the time. I was unaware that there is such a thing as spiritual darkness. Little did I know that I was being initiated into a cult which was to have far reaching results on my life.

As I passed through the degrees I discovered that I was aware of evil for the first time and I began to live in fear. In particular I remember being buried wrapped up in a black flag emblazoned with skull and cross bones as part of one of the rituals. (This is approaching the climax of the third degree, that of the Master Mason - Ed.). Although I made no pretence of being religious, rather the contrary, I found this spooky and how ever much I tried the awareness of evil did not go away over the years.

Also from about this time everything began to go wrong. Having been very healthy I started to have one illness after another: virus infections, nervous troubles and finally a diagnosis of trigeminal neuralgia - sometimes known as tic-douloureux. The latter was confirmed at St. Bartholomew's hospital in 1978 when I was told that I would be on drugs for the rest of my life. Relationships became increasingly more difficult until I even wanted to leave my wife and children. In short, my life was a complete mess and the fellowship provided by the Freemasons was quite unable to provide any help. I resigned.

On 14/12/80 I went to my local Parish Church in despair. There I listened to what was said about Jesus Christ. I heard that we all have sinned and fallen short of the Glory of God, but if I would come to this Jesus, who was crucified because of my sins, I would be accepted as a child. Then because Jesus Christ overcame death and evil by rising from the tomb, I would be given new life. I sat and thought about all of this and when the congregation went forward to take Holy Communion I went with them. Whilst kneeling on the chancel step I addressed Almighty God; not a Grand Architect of the Universe or Geometrician or any other god used in Freemasonry. There I renounced my former way of life, asked for forgiveness of all my sins, forgave all those I hated and asked to be fed with the Bread of Life. Immediately I was transported from darkness into a glorious light. I left the Church a new man, forgiven and healed. I have not taken nor needed drugs since that day. Praise God!

Something I did not realise at the time I went through the initiation rituals into Freemasonry was the sin I committed against God. I bowed the knee as it says in the Bible, yes, on one knee with feet placed in the form of an occult symbol, to a god I did not know. There is no mention of Jesus Christ, the only Son of the Living God or the blood of Jesus in the degrees I passed through. Free-masonry breaks the first Commandment and its rituals are idolatrous and pagan.

For about two years I seemed to live on "cloud nine". Then as more people began to hear about what had happened I was asked to speak publicly on this experience. However I soon discovered that I had another problem. Sometimes and often without warning, I found myself unable to pray for other people in need. It was just as if I was tied down by a tremendous opposing force. On occasions the presence of evil in my house was so intense that I wondered if I were going insane. One day I asked God in prayer to show me the cause of the trouble.

Very soon afterwards I was invited to a prayer meeting at 08.00 hours one Tuesday morning in the City of London. I really thought it was a joke and had no intention of attending, but when the time came I was there - and early into the bargain. Only two other people turned up at the start and a complete stranger began to talk about the time when Jesus raised Lazarus from the dead. He explained that when Lazarus walked out from the tomb he was wearing grave clothes. In other words he was alive but restricted in movement, as if his arms and legs were wound about with bandages. I was reminded that Jesus commanded His disciples to release him and let him go. This I was told is part of the work of God's Church to-day and we could be bound up like Lazarus without being aware of the reason why.

Thinking I would be smart I asked this stranger for some "for instances". He paused, looked at the ceiling and said:-

"If, for instance, somebody had had an affair, perhaps before becoming a Christian and tucked at the back of the top left hand drawer in a desk at the office were love notes, cards or presents from that relationship that would be like grave clothes."

I think I probably rubbed the hair on the back of my neck but, undaunted, I asked for another "for instance". At this point the man replied quietly that masonic regalia and ritual books hidden away, maybe in the wardrobe at home, would be like grave clothes. I could not take any more and admitted to having all the things mentioned and I asked for guidance as to what I must do.

With love and gentleness I was taught, with appropriate references to Holy Scripture, that I had bowed the knee to Baal. As I was unable to take immediate steps to deal with the offending material it was agreed that I should see my Vicar as soon as possible. In the meantime those present laid hands on me and prayed that I and my family would be protected from all harm by the blood of Jesus. I was also warned to be on guard against a piritual onslaught. In particular I was advised to behave as Jesus had instructed His disciples when He sent them out and to say whenever I entered my home:-

"Peace be to this house."

not to the people in the house but to the building as it were. Some days later, after renouncing my involvement in Freemasonry and with praise to

Almighty God for delivering me from this evil, the regalia, insignia and ritual books were burned.

Truly I now know the Peace of God which passes all understanding. Daily I give thanks and praise to God that by His Grace I have been set free!

Chapter 10

The Testimony of Roy Farran

I WAS a partner in a firm of consulting engineers when I was first approached to join a Lodge. It was indicated that this was the way to promote my professional activities, but the circumstances did not seem appropriate and the offer lapsed.

Later I was approached by a long standing business associate who clearly considered I would enjoy the companionship of like-minded men. In this case there were no overtones of business advantage and I was invited to meet one or two members of the Lodge and to join on the basis that they were representatives of good, moral men who would not be involved in anything wrong. I was further assured that I would find nothing in Freemasonry that would offend my religion.

At the time of joining the Lodge I was a Christian of the evangelical tradition and had been for many years, although latterly I had allowed my personal commitment to Christ to wear very thin. I could see no reason theologically for not joining, although I became somewhat uneasy at the various initiation ceremonies. However, many churchmen are members and most Lodges have chaplains and any misgivings were easily overcome, particularly as a senior mason advised me not to take the ritual too seriously. Besides, my new companions were good company and in general moral and upright men as I had been led to expect. In addition several charitable activities were well supported by members.

What went wrong? Some four years after joining I was under increasing pressures from illness and stress to an extent that I had to face the apparent inevitability of enforced retirement from professional life. It was at this low point that I began to seek afresh that first encounter with the Lord Jesus Christ who came to save from all the consequences of sin. For the first time I realised that the word "save" covered not only spirit, but body and soul as well.

A direct result of an evangelistic meeting, in which the power of Jesus to completely save was proclaimed, was an immediate release from illness and its side effects. That was in 1981, and I have no plans for retirement yet!

The release of Jesus' healing power led to a desire to accept all that God offers in His Word and this was followed quickly by asking for, and receiving by faith, the infilling of the Holy Spirit described in Acts Chapter Two. This experience led, amongst other things, to a gradual but increasing awareness that Freemasonry is incompatible with Christianity, when it is based upon the Bible as the inspired Word of God.

Inexorably a deeper understanding of the Word of God has shown that many of the practices in the Lodge are wrong - the oath taking; the general secrecy; the denial of Jesus Christ, whilst acknowledging the "great architect of the universe". This latter practice opens the door to gods other than the one true God and reveals the occult nature of many of the mysteries contained in Freemasonry.

All of this is in contradiction to the Word of God and having made the decision to leave, I explained my difficulty to my original sponsor, an officer in the Grand Lodge who with his thirty years experience in the Craft agreed that a personal commitment to Jesus Christ could only become more and more incompatible with Freemasonry as progression in the Craft was achieved. How sad for a man so entrenched in Freemasonry to have the wisdom to see for himself this truth and yet be incapable of applying it in his own life.

Subsequent experience in counselling those in Freemasonry but wishing to leave and serve the Lord Jesus Christ has shown how insidious and deceptive the devil is in drawing men step by step, in what seems at first harmless ways, into the grip of Freemasonry.

However, those who persevere find that He Who is in them is greater than he who is in the world, and obtain a complete release into the light which only faith in the Lord Jesus Christ can provide.

Chapter 11

Masons and Clergy

BEING a copy of a letter from Canon G. B. Bentley to The Times and published on 14.9.84 and reproduced with his permission.

Sir, A good many years ago a reasoned motion was tabled in the Lower House of the Canterbury Convocation expressing disquiet about the involvement of clergymen in Masonry and calling for an inquiry. Its sponsors feared, inter alia, that commitment to a secret brotherhood could impair a pastor's relationship with the non-Masons in his cure.

Unhappy with the complexity of this motion, I tabled an amendment that simply asked for the appointment of a joint committee to consider and report on the matter.

This is what happened. When the time came for the Proprolocutor who was in the chair that day (a Mason) ruled the reasoned motion out of order, whereupon I put forward my amendment in its place. On that being reported to the Archbishop (another Mason) he urged the Proprolocutor to see that it was quashed. I had that on the testimony of a person who was in the Upper House at the time.

When my motion was reached, our Masonic chairman informed me that I could put it, but not make my speech! I declined to move on those terms and the motion lapsed. I should, of course, have contested the ruling, but I was too flabbergasted to collect my wits in time. After the session pressmen present commented to me on the patent antagonism of the Chair.

Subsequently I had some correspondence with the Archbishop, who promised that a request for an inquiry would be moved during the next group of sessions of the Church Assembly and assured me that that would clear the matter up.

Sure enough, the then Vicar of Windsor (another Mason) did move for an inquiry, but in the same breath called on the Assembly to reject it out of hand. When afterwards the Archbishop wrote to ask if I was now satisfied, I replied that, on the contrary, I thought the whole affair stank.

That experience taught me all I needed to know about Masonry.

Yours faithfully,

G. B. Bentley.

Chapter 12

The Testimony of the Reverend W. E. Howe

TRYING to find "light" in my early thirties, I was drawn to the Church - it had been around for a long while so there must be something in it - and also to Freemasonry which had intrigued me for some time, though I knew little about it or the Church either come to that.

I saw no inconsistancy in this dual approach particularly as I was told that some Bishops were also Freemasons and I soon found there was a canon as chaplain of the lodge I was to join, which stopped any doubts arising.

Within a short while I found myself newly confirmed by the Bishop and newly initiated into Freemasonry, but keeping up my attendance at lodge, whilst failing to be faithful in worship.

I thought that I was being faithful in my Lodge attendance to which I was obligated, but not in public worship which depended on my free response to God.

The upshot of this was that I made my own obligation to go to Holy Communion at 7 a.m. on the day of my Lodge meeting, which I faithfully did with the result that after some months I became a regular and active Church member.

I must emphasise how pivotal this decision was

because looking back I firmly believe God used that time of obedience and following the truth as I saw it to prepare me for something in the future which also took me out of Freemasonry.

I found fellowship and friendship in the Lodge, perhaps more so than in Church, with men like myself drawn to wherever it was leading us. There was some mutual help in business matters but as far as I know, no more than in any other grouping of people coming together for a common purpose.

A few things began to stand out against Christianity; the Old Testament ethos, lack of flexibility (I would now put it in terms of "life"), the manner and scope of giving to charity, but particularly the limitations of commitment.

Jesus gave His life and called His followers to deny themselves, a course of action detrimental to oneself and one's connections, something not called for in Freemasonry.

True I had not gone very far forward, some told me there was a Christian dimension further on but perhaps intuitively I decided this would be far enough for me and no further.

Very soon I had to take a decision which affected my whole life, including my family. Because through a comment made to me in jest, I got the notion of being ordained - an idea that was hilarious to my friends and myself, but wouldn't go away.

After a traumatic time lasting some years I went away to a theological college for two years leaving my wife at home with the family. Even then I kept in contact with Freemasonry attending a local lodge as a guest, still without any sense of incongruity, more as a subsidiary interest.

It was only three years or more after ordination that I began to see these two things, Christianity and Freemasonry in perspective and decided I must be cut free from the latter if I was to be free to follow Jesus Christ, for such things have a spiritual hold.

I can now put it in language that I could not have used in earlier days.

Symbolism and allegory had always had an attraction for me and there is plenty of those in Freemasonry, but in Christianity allegory and symbols are essentially subsidiary pointers to an historical Person who took flesh and blood, died and was raised from death for mankind, God's chosen means of salvation.

We are meant for fellowship with God our Father mediated through Jesus Who said He is the only Way.

You cannot have a personal relationship with allegory and symbols or with a system of morality, but you can with a Person who is alive and makes Himself known though He is beyond all knowledge.

God has revealed all we need to know and can know of himself in Jesus Christ, there are no secrets held back to be doled out by degrees, living water flows for all who will drink, male and female, young and old.

Any other teaching must be darkness and allegiance to it is a denial of the true light that at a particular time and place came into and is still in the world.

I have no wish to attack Freemasons who may have been drawn in perhaps as I was. I believe there is no justification for "exposures", though a lot can be done on a one - to - one basis with those who have been involved. I have made my peace with God over the ceremonies I went through and pray that He will in His mercy do for others what graciously He did for me. I hope that telling my story might help.

"And if the Spirit of Him Who raised Jesus from the dead is living in you, He Who raised Christ from the dead will also give life to your mortal bodies through His Spirit Who lives in you." (Romans 8: 11 N.I.V.)

What do we need more?

W. Howe.

Chapter 13

The Evidence of
Two Policemen

THE view of Inspector M.J.Salts.

Few thinking police officers and even fewer members of the public would seek to dispense with the Police Regulation that deals with "Restrictions on the Private Life of Members" (see Reg.4 and the 1st. Schedule). Indeed a careful consideration of its contents reveals that it is an essential adjunct to the British Constitution; for surely it is vital that:-

"A member of a Police Force shall at all times abstain from any activity which is likely to interfere with the impartial discharge of his duties, or which is likely to give rise to the impression amongst members of the public that it may so interfere....."

And yet surrepticiously there is in our midst a sprinkling of men who are in flagrant breach of that Regulation. I refer to those officers who have forsaken their original vow of impartiality and taken an unholy oath of allegiance to a secret body called "Freemasons".

Now most Freemasons have long since convinced themselves that there is nothing wrong in what they do. Their Lodge Meetings appear to be quite innocuous. If they wear their aprons and insignia and practise their meaningful handshakes and ancient rituals why should we object?

We find no fault in those particular things. But we feel bound to draw attention to the fact that the Freemasons' oath puts a police officer's impartiality in jeopardy. We pose the question:-

"How can a police officer remain impartial in the matter of duty if he has taken a solemn oath which compels him to favour, against all others, those who have taken the same oath?"

It is hardly any wonder that Freemasonry is cloaked in secrecy. If the present day Masons could take an objective view of themselves they would realise that the worthy principles of their early forebears are no longer maintained and the lodges are peopled by those whose interest is entirely selfish.

How often do we hear of men being promoted who are decidedly not the best men for the job? How often is seniority disregarded in favour of a man who has paid a "sub" and taken the Masons' oath? How many police officers in Freemasonry have been invited to "turn a blind eye" because a fellow Mason has broken the law? What happens to a man's integrity after he has taken an unholy oath?

There are Freemasons in all ranks of the police service. But they have to keep quiet about it because they know that as Masons they cannot comply with the spirit of the Police Regulations.

Beware of Freemasonry! It is better by far to maintain your integrity than to sell it for the hope of early promotion.

This is included here as an actual example of the concern expressed by Inspector M.J. Salts.

Personal Experiences of Det. Sgt. F. Smith rtd.

HE writes:-

"I was a Detective Constable with 7 years service when one night as I came back into the Station about 1 am. I was telephoned by my Deputy Chief Constable who instructed me to pick him up at his club. This was not unusual when he had spent the evening at a hotel or club. I took him home and as we went into his house he said:-

"You know about the three monkeys don't you Smith?"

"Yes sir, Good night."

The following morning I was summoned into his office when he congratulated me on the efficient way I carried out my duties adding that both he and the Chief Constable had been watching me recently as they were about to transfer my Detective Inspector back into uniform and they were looking for a replacement. He told me that he had informed the Chief that I had more "know how" in my little finger than my D/I had in his whole body adding:-

"so we have decided to promote you to the rank of Det. Sergeant to take over H.Q.-C.I.D."

I was not only surprised but elated as 40 years ago it was normal to wait between 12 to 15 years for promotion to Sergeant in any department, Traffic, Admin, C.I.D. or whatever.

He told me to report to the Administration Inspector the following day for my chevrons to put on my uniform (all plain clothes officers had also to have a proper set of uniform) saying that the promotion would be published in the Force General Orders the next day. As I turned to leave the office he said:-

"By the way Smith, you are on the square aren't you?"

"No sir."

"But surely your father is?"

I knew only too well that it was almost necessary to be a member of the Freemasons in our Force before you could gain promotion and I could see mine going out of the window so I lied and said that I didn't know. My father had told me before I left home to join the Force that if I ever joined the Masons I was never to come home again. As this was going through my mind the next question came:-

"but you will become a Mason won't you?"

Suddenly I was angry inside and thought that even if the promotion was on merit the rest of the fellows would not believe me that I hadn't joined so I simply said:-

"I had no intention of joining, then or ever."

to which came the rejoinder:-

"Forget everything I have said to you, dismiss."

I had to wait another 12 years until both the Chief and Deputy Chief had retired, when a new Chief arrived from the North of England. I was the first one he promoted....after 19 years of service.

This wasn't the only unfortunate encounter with the Masonic movement. When I had served 14 years the Chief Inspector in charge of the H.Q.

Traffic Department....bless him he was NOT a Mason and a nicer man I have never served with....he knew all about my lost promotion years earlier and he sent for me one day and said :-

"Would you mind leaving the C.I.D. if it meant your promotion?"

to which I naturally said:-

"No sir, but why do you ask?"

He then told me that Her Majesty's Inspector of Constabularies had, at his last Force Inspection, recommended that there should be an additional Sergeant in the Traffic Department and he said he would very much like me to have it so he recommended me. Again I got quite excited at the prospect as the Sergeants' rank is the hardest to get as there are hundreds who have qualified by passing their Promotion Examination so the odds are far greater than they are for relatively few Sergeants to Inspector.

My refusal to become a Mason had not been forgotten however and it was given to a P.C. who was a Mason. Within 2 years he was promoted Inspector, 1 year later on to Superintendent and 3 years later to Assistant Chief Constable and I thought "there goes me" if I'd been one, however the end is not so happy as he died within a year. There were MANY very good Constables who retired without promotion yet they were far more worthy than many who went up the tree.

In conclusion let me say what I said many times when I was a serving member of the Force. The benefits and lifestyle and the education of my children depended on my promotion. On leaving the service any prospective employer wanted to know what rank you held thinking it was indicative of your ability which was totally untrue. So the Masons get the "plums" after retirement as well as in the Force.

As a Christian I have been able to forgive them but prior to my conversion I held a bitterness that was common to very good men who never had a chance to prove themselves.

I purposely haven't named names, many are dead now and I've forgiven them anyway."

Fred Smith lives in Abingdon and is one of the pastors of a Fellowship. God has given to him an exciting ministry of healing.

Chapter 14

Is Freemasonry Counterfeit?

THUS far this book has been concerned with the testimonies of men like myself who, for one reason or another, have been made Masons.

For varying periods of time we have sat in Lodge. We have "progressed", undertaking the various offices and duties that are open to keen and aspiring Freemasons. Irrespective of why we sought to be initiated into the Craft there came a moment in all of our lives when God spoke to each one of us in differing ways. To Ron Price He spoke quite categorically, to me so gently that I was outside Freemasonry before I began to realise its true demonic nature. The overall results were our resignations. No collusion or premeditation has taken place yet the stories, including my own, have a remarkable similarity.

It seems to me that the receiving the Baptism of the Holy Spirit and the office of Junior Warden have been of especial significance. The reason for the first is pretty obvious, but what about the second point? Is it because it is the first of the trinity of officers who rule the Lodge? Is there some especial blasphemous content in the offices of Worshipful Master and his two Wardens? If there is anything specific in them I am still unaware of it.

One aspect we all have in common is, like John Newton in "Amazing Grace", once we were lost, but now we are found, were blind but now we see! It still thrills me that after re-renouncing and re-repenting of my Masonic incursion including my wife Mary that we could then, and have continued to, pray together!

Chapter 15

"Christ his Witness, the Great Architect his guide."

THE Freemason Dean of St. Albans explains his apparently conflicting beliefs to Pat Krett.
(Extracted from "The Times" of 25/8/84)

Joining the Freemasons has always posed special problems for churchmen because of the Masons' refusal to acknowledge Christ's divinity and concern about the nature of the God(s) to which they give allegiance. The publication earlier this year of Stephen Knight's "The Brotherhood" merely refuelled the centuries-old anxieties.

Senior clergy who are Freemasons have shown a marked reluctance to come out into the open and defend their position. But now the Dean of St. Albans, the Very Rev. Peter Moore, a high ranking Mason, has spoken about the misunderstandings which he feels that the movement's secrecy has helped to generate.

Dr. Moore, who is 60, has been the Dean of St. Albans for 11 years and a Mason since 1950. On the issue of the Masons' two ceremonies of commitment at which the existance of a deity is acknowledged, but - confusingly - different names are used. Dr. Moore revealed that leading Masons themselves are divided. It is this ceremony, discussed in Knight's book in a chapter entitled "The Devil in disguise?", which causes many of the misgivings because it is difficult, as he discovered, to get a coherent and consistent definition of who exactly this deity is, and represents.

According to Knight this god is JAH-BUL-ON. And he claims that it is a "specific supernatural being", made up of three separate personalities, two of them pagan. The Dean, while denying the suggestion that there is any worship of the occult in Freemasonry, said that he withdrew from rites where this word is invoked.

"I do that because I think that particular word is nonsense. And I am not alone. This matter has been raised at the highest levels within Freemasonry. But nothing has happened about it. It is contentious without unpleasantness."

On first being accepted into the ranks of Masonry, all recruits have to pledge their belief, in a solemn ceremony, to a god called "The Great Architect of the Universe." This is the first sticking point in the acceptance of Masonry for many Christians. But Dr. Moore feels that the unfamiliar words, secrecy about the rituals and traditional unwillingness by Masons to discuss the movement with outsiders have resulted in serious misunderstandings.

He said: "Masonry is not a religion and specifically says it isn't. I think, on the other hand, for some people who would otherwise have nothing, it gives them something. And it is one of the bases of Freemasonry that you accept the existence of the

Great Architect of the Universe. This is God, though not in the Christian sense. The God that we worship is the same God that Jews and Muslims worship. It is God. There can be only one God."

While sympathising with those Christians who feel that they could not belong to a body that excluded the recognition of Christ's divinity, he said that it was not an issue of conscience for him: "Some people feel that their allegiance to Christ is compromised by associating with people who accept God but not Christ. I don't feel like that. I am glad to be associated with people who accept God as Creator."

And he stressed that he saw no conflict between his Christian belief and commitments and his Masonry membership: "I have no doubt at all what my top priority is - which is my job as Dean - which is my life."

Dr. Moore has risen to high rank in both the Church and Freemasonry. He at one time held office as Grand Chaplain of Grand Lodge, the London-based top tier of Masonry. But he emphasised that being a Mason had in no way helped him in his Church career.

He joined when a chaplain at New College, Oxford, attracted by the movement's mystique and because a number of his friends were members: "the element of secrecy in it interests one. You want to know why."

A few years ago he started an annual service in St. Albans for Freemasons, with agreement of the Chapter. This year's, held last Sunday (21.10.84 -

Ed.), attracted a congregation of about 300 Masons and their wives.

Did a Masonic service have any special features, I asked Dr. Moore. He said no Masonic insignia would be worn, nor any changes made to the Cathedral decor, though he admitted that in the past some bizarre things had been allowed elsewhere which had generated concern:

"In the bad old days extraordinary things were done. For instance there are tales of the cross being removed from churches because the Masons had a service. But I have nothing to do with that sort of thing. Anyone who comes to worship in the cathedral does what we do".

I attended the service, and the only part that jarred was the description in the closing prayers given by the Rev. Dr. Robert MacQueen, a former G.P. and now rector of Royston, Hertfordshire, to heaven as "The Great Grand Lodge above".

Dr. Moore and Dr. MacQueen later assured me that there was no Freemasonry in Heaven. It was a Masonic synonym.

The origins of the special vocabulary and sometimes bloodcurdling oaths of the Craft is in part an accident of history, said Dr.Moore: "Masonry got going at the beginning of the eighteenth century in England - a period of allegory. If we started to-day we shouldn't start with a lot of the things that exist."

Various unpleasant and even fatal penalties are accepted in a solemn ceremony as the punishment for anyone who betrays the Brotherhood's clandestine codes. The tongue and heart to be torn out and the bowels burned to ashes.

But this was not intended to be taken literally, said Dr. Moore. "These are the traditional penalties. I have never heard of them being used. If I really thought that was going to happen I would pack up tomorrow."

Dr. Moore pointed out that Masonry raised large sums for charities, and no longer exclusively their own. The often heard complaint that they "feathered their own nests" had been heeded and there had been radical changes.

The St. Albans Abbey restoration appeal for £1.7m has benefitted by a £5,000 donation from Grand Lodge.

He also made it clear that one of the valued aspects of Masonry for him, and many others, is the comradeship it offers. He explained: "I can go to any part of the country, any town anywhere, and will be welcomed in the lodge without reservation. It enables me to meet a cross section of the community whom I should otherwise never meet."

Chapter 16

Some Comments on Chapter 15

BEFORE we return to a general discussion perhaps we could take a look at one point that the Dean raises. He said that he withdrew from rites where this word "JAH-BUL-ON" is invoked. In the ritual of the Holy Royal Arch, where this name is introduced, it is explained that this is the secret of the master mason which was lost by the untimely death of Hiram Abiff. Even if the word is not actually spoken in the three introductory degrees they are leading towards it. If, as he suggests, this word is nonsense then surely the steps leading to its revelation are equally nonsensical. Also, is there any validity in any of the succeeding degrees? Any structure erected upon such a foundation cannot be worthy and true. Thus the whole fabric of Freemasonry could be considered to be foolishness and void of import from the serious and open consideration of just this one composite name.

It is not as simple as that. Freemasonry does not set out to be just a "businessmen's" club. The main qualification prior to initiation is the belief in some Supreme Spiritual Being. This being so, the Craft is brought into direct conflict with the God of the Old Testament Who declared that we should not have any other god but Him or besides Him. It is just not good enough to say that He is the same God, for in the New Testament Jesus declares that He is the only way to the Father, the God of Abraham, Isaac and Jacob.

Obviously Freemasons are all still quite happy with their continuing membership, otherwise they would be like me and have resigned. I believe that one can only be extricated from Freemasonry by the power of God the Holy Spirit in the name of Jesus.

Chapter 17

A Review of the First Degree

TESTING the spirits is a perfectly good spiritual exercise. Even at the time when John wrote his three Epistles some time towards the end of the first century A.D., he found it necessary to instruct his readers to do just that. I find his first letter especially helpful. For example I quote 1 John: 3 v.1-3:-

"Beloved, do not believe every spirit, but test the spirits to see whether they are from God; because many false prophets have gone out into the world.

By this you know the Spirit of God: every spirit that confesses that Jesus Christ has come in the flesh is from God;

and every spirit that does not confess Jesus is not from God; and this is the spirit of antichrist, of which you have heard that it is coming, and now it is already in the world."

These words, written by John the Apostle nearly nineteen centuries ago according to many scholars, give us to-day a salutary warning if taken seriously. If Satan is real, if he is setting himself against Almighty God, if he is endeavouring to build a kingdom for himself, then one fact is obvious; to achieve any success in this direction his counterfeiting must be superb. He must present his wares most attractively, the trappings and wrappings must be so enticing in order that the unsuspecting soul is caught; a spider and fly situation. If the fly realised its ultimate fate before encountering the web, would it be caught?

Please bear in mind that it was over thirty years ago when I was initiated into Freemasonry, and some twenty years since my resignations from the various Lodges. In retrospect I am amazed that I was a very keen member and "brother" right from the first degree, but this was so. All the people with whom I came into contact were sympathetic, helpful and encouraging, as I indeed tried to be towards them and the newer initiates who followed me through the ceremonies. Friendliness certainly was one of the main characteristics of the Lodge meetings and also of the banquets that followed. But what was this Masonic Secret that motivated them - and me?

The ceremonies - rituals - were performed with quite a degree of solemnity. This I found impressive and somehow satisfying, certainly at first. Early in my Masonic career I was appointed the Lodge Organist and I tried to select music to suit these occasions. This was not too difficult for most of my little experience in music had been at the church organ console. On one evening the Director of Ceremonies - the officer responsible for rehearsals and for the smooth working within the Lodge - suggested that I "jazzed the music up a bit". This is quite a simple point in itself, but it came about at the time I had been delivered from demonic bondage of spiritism and had had those satanic blinkers removed. This awakening awareness was a very gradual process, but I began to see a pointlessness creep into my Masonic working. Where was it all leading? More and more of the ritual had to be memorised but the object of the exercise seemed to be ever farther away. I suppose if I had been content to be a Master Mason only and not to want to climb up the ladder of advancement I might have stayed a member of the Craft for many more years. It is an attractive thought to respond to the discipline to attend Lodge, sit through the workings on the floor, and then, if there is no other business of personal interest, repair to the banquetting hall to round off a peaceful, relaxing evening. Because the Lodge is securely "tyled" there can be no interruptions from the busy business world outside the door, a convenient form of escapism....... However this is idle speculation, for the Lord dealt with me so gently that it was some time after I had severed completely all Masonic ties to my wife and to me that I began to realise the real truth about the Brotherhood. Who am I to suggest that the Lord might have left me any longer in the Craft for whatever reason; He is Lord! His will is sovereign.

Two points that are often expressed by masons about Freemasonry to those who are not members are:-

(a) it is not a religion, and

(b) only in the Masonic Lodge can the true significance of the ceremonies be appreciated.

Chambers Twentieth Century Dictionary begins

its definition of "RELIGION" thus:-

"belief in, recognition of, or an awakened sense of, a higher unseen controlling power or powers, with the emotion and morality connected therewith: rites or worship: any system of such belief or worship......"

To me, now, this describes Freemasonry; for in the first degree reference is made to The Great Architect of the Universe (T.G.A.O.T.U.), in the second to the Grand Geometrician, and in the third degree to the Most High. The rites and ceremonies are so orientated. The senior colleague whom I had asked if he would guide me about Freemasonry and who actually proposed me, asked me one question and one question only before he actually put my name forward to the standing committee of the Lodge and this was about my belief in a Supreme Being. This surprised me at the time for he knew of my attendance and of commitment to the Church of England. We were both churchwardens but in different parishes.

Freemasonry has a spiritual content, a supernatural implication, for reference is made to "ascending from this subluminary abode to the Grand Lodge above." Does this mean that Salvation is from the earthly Masonic Temple to, what the non-mason might consider as, eternal life in Heaven? It is of little comfort to an Initiate to hear and to be prompted to say words, especially in the solemn yet horrific obligations, if their interpretations are substantially different from that in common usage outside the door of the Lodge. Again, in the Craft the rituals and allegories are objects of themselves, but in Christianity Jesus uses the parable, not as an end in itself, but as a pointer to some spiritual truth not readily understood by His audience.

Let us come to the Candidate for Initiation as he is prepared to be made a Mason. First he is divested of all monies and metallic substances of value - all his pockets are emptied except for a handkerchief - but he is allowed to retain a pair of reading spectacles. His jacket is taken off and his shirt is unbuttoned down to the waist and thus his left breast is made bare. One trouser leg is rolled up to the knee, whilst the shoe on the other foot is removed and replaced by a slipper which has no heel. Now a "cable tow" - that is, a running noose - is placed round his neck. Finally he is blindfolded, the "hoodwink" is put in position.

Thus arrayed - maybe "disarrayed" might be the better term - the attention of the Inner Guard is drawn by the Tyler who knocks a pre-arranged signal on the Lodge door. The Candidate's presence is now officially proclaimed by the Tyler to the Inner Guard as:-

"Mr. David Vaughan, a poor candidate in a state of darkness who has been well and worthily recommended, regularly approved in open lodge and now comes of his own free will and accord, properly prepared, humbly soliciting to be admitted to the mysteries and privileges of Freemasonry"

if my memory serves me well. The door of the Lodge was then closed and locked whilst the same announcement was made by the Inner Guard to the Worshipful Master who then ordered that I

"be admitted in due form."

The door of the Temple was now opened and I was allowed to go just inside. A brief ceremony ensued during which I was asked:-

"Do you feel anything?"

and was told to say

"Yes".

Then the Junior Deacon, as I later discovered him to be, led me on a perambulation round the Lodge being introduced in a similar way to the Junior and Senior Wardens in turn as "a poor candidate etc. etc." Then I was led to the place of the Worshipful Master who demanded of me if was I a free man and of the full age of twenty-one years. After assuring the Worshipful Master that I was indeed free and over the age of twenty-one years I was told to kneel at his pedestal, to turn my feet out in the form of a square

"whilst the blessing of heaven is invoked upon what we are about to do".

This comforted me tremendously for Heaven is whence Jesus reigns and I had had my faith in Him confirmed many years previously by the Bishop of Stafford. I had meant business on that occasion and although I had wandered very far from the Truth, and was to go even further away, I had not rejected Him, but in my heart He was still My Lord!

The invocation which followed was directed to "Almighty Father and Supreme Governor of the Universe", an indication of the masonic concept, which is developed later, that God is not unique as

He would be, of necessity, if He were the Creator. Later in the same supplication comes:-

"......so that assisted by the secrets of our masonic art he may be the better enabled to unfold the beauties of true godliness...."

Compare this with the words of Jesus that Luke records for us in chapter 12 v.3:-

"But there is nothing covered up that will not be revealed, and hidden that will not be known. Accordingly, whatever you have said in the dark shall be heard in the light, and what you have whispered in the inner rooms shall be proclaimed from the housetops."

It was in this position that the horrendous obligation was administered. In retrospect, I wonder now whether I would have taken that oath if I had not recognised the voice of the Worshipful Master as that of a Director of the company that employed me.

When I had taken the obligation of "an Entered Apprentice Freemason" I was asked what was the predominant desire of my heart. The blindfold was still in place so it did not take much prompting to say:-

"Light."

In response to the Worshipful Master's command:-

"Let that blessing be restored to the Candidate."

The hoodwink was removed adroitly and straight in front of my eyes was an open copy of the Holy Bible, a masonic version as I was later to discover. The pages were held open by a small silver set square and pair of dividers, but at what page I never did discover. Later I was informed that that was irrelevant according to masonic principles, but that it was the whole Book that was one of the great lights of Freemasonry. Never did I read anything from that particular copy, nor did I ever see anyone else read from Scripture within the Lodge.

Now I was able to see my new brethren, who had just accepted me as a new duly obligated brother among Masons, and to recognise some of them. Of course it was exciting to be welcomed into such a fellowship; the novelty of it all helped me to allay my concern over Jesus' words in Matthew: 5 v 34-37:-

"....make no oath at all but let your statement be 'Yes, yes' or 'No, no'. and anything beyond these is of the evil one."

Yet it was this command that I had broken and was continuing to break. Did the knowledge that Kings and Archbishops had taken these selfsame steps help me to dull my conscience and stifle my belief in the Holy Bible as the inerrant Word of God? Possibly, but that is no excuse! Proceeding on through the ceremony, the horrific nature to what I had committed myself soon began to fade.

The Worshipful Master began to explain some of the details of my preparation. He asked me to contribute some money towards some worthy cause, but having nothing disposable on my person I was precluded from so doing. When asked if I would have done so were I able, I agreed that I would. This was to remind me that I was poor and indigent when I was received into Freemasonry so that, if I were ever to meet in the future a brother Mason in that plight, then I should cheerfully embrace the opportunity to help.

What of the cable tow and the open shirt front? Why were these necessary? My exposed chest enabled the Inner Guard to "present a poniard to my naked left breast" such that if I had rashly rushed forward I would have been stabbed to death if the Inner Guard had "stood firm and done his duty". On the other hand, if I had decided to turn tail and flee, the Tyler would have held the end of the running noose thus rendering escape impossible. In any case, with one foot being slipshod (dictionary definitions include "slovenly"), walking was not too easy let alone running. But what an introduction to the Brotherhood, an Institution that is based, allegedly, on:-

"brotherly love, relief and truth".

I was assured that all this was necessary to ensure that:-

"the mysteries and privileges were reserved for worthy men and for worthy men alone."

Compare this to the Holy Bible which tells us that the reason why Jesus came was to save sinners - and to destroy the works of the Devil - and to make Life available to us in abundance. John 10:10

Paul deals with the former point in his first letter to Timothy: 1. v.15:-

"It is a trustworthy statement, deserving full acceptance, that Christ Jesus came into the world to save sinners, among whom I am foremost of all."

And John in his first letter chapter 3 v. 7,8:-

"Little children, let no one deceive you; the one who practices righteousness is righteous, just as He is righteous;

the one who practices sin is of the devil; for the devil has sinned from the beginning. The Son of God appeared for this purpose, that He might destroy the works of the devil."

Upon reflection, was this bizarre beginning to the ceremony of initiation responsible for the further dulling of those sensibilities towards Jesus that I had retained?

"Was I a free man and of the full age of twenty-one years?"
the Worshipful Master had asked me. Shades of Lord Wilberforce - slavery had been abolished in the British Empire some two hundred years ago and I was middle-aged. For a worldly society these two provisos might seem reasonable. Perhaps "free" might mean that I was not an escaped convict on the run from the Police. As regards the age of majority I wonder if the "Antient" ritual has been altered to eighteen years in the mid Nineteen-eighties?

It is quite futile to pursue these lines of thought for the Bible, proclaimed as one of the great lights of Freemasonry, is quite blunt and forthright on these two points. In Jesus there is only one classification:-

"For by one Spirit we were all baptised into one body, whether Jews or Greeks, whether slaves or free, and we were all made to drink of the one Spirit." (I Cor: 12: 13)
also:-

"there is neither Jew nor Greek, there is neither slave nor freeman, there is neither male nor female, for all are one in Christ Jesus." (Gal: 3 v.28.)

and later at Gal: 4 v.26 we read:-

"But the Jerusalem above is free...."

Jesus died to pay the debt incurred by the sins of each individual person in the world, and by coming to Jesus alone can anyone be saved. As Peter is reported in Acts: 4 v.12:-

"And there is salvation in no one else, for there is no other name under heaven that has been given among men by which we must be saved."

There are many references to little children, from the mouth of Jesus Himself. Take, for example:-

"Truly I say to you, unless you are converted and become like children, you shall not enter the kingdom of heaven."
(Mat: 18 v. 3)

and in verse 4 of the same chapter:-

"Whoever then humbles himself as this little child, he is the greatest in the kingdom of heaven."

"But Jesus said:- 'Let the children alone, and do not hinder them from coming to Me, for the kingdom of heaven belongs to such as these.'" (Mat: 19 v.14.)

In John: 3 v.3 is recorded a very blunt statement in reply to Nicodemus, a leading Pharisee:-

"Jesus answered and said to him:- "Truly, truly I say to you, unless one is born again he cannot see the kingdom of God.""

Note that Jesus prefaces this answer by "truly,

truly" or "verily, verily". In other words, as Jesus spoke truthfully always, is He implying here that what He is saying here is true even if you have difficulty in accepting it as such?

Mortal maturity and rectitude are of no consequence whatsoever. Indeed Isaiah recorded for us in chapter 64: 6:-

".....And all our righteous deeds are like a filthy garment...."

The Authorised Version is more descriptive for it uses the term "filthy rags."

Thus, according to Scripture we can do nothing of ourselves that is worth anything in the sight of our heavenly Father. How we assess ourselves is totally irrelevant when considered from the aspect of eternity. Yet the Entered Apprentice is placed standing in the north-east corner of the Lodge emblematically to represent a corner stone, upon which he is adjured to build a structure, worthy and beautiful in its proportions.

Where does Freemasonry fit into this picture? What are the Masonic Arts that assist in the unfolding of true godliness? I had hopes of finding out something about this during my first evening as an Entered Apprentice Freemason. During the fifteen years I spent as a Freemason I discovered nothing in the Craft. Not one step did I make towards the godliness which seemed so attractive, so imminent on that first night. The novelty, the excitement crumbled into dust as soon as I began to think seriously and lucidly about what I was doing. I was a married man with a loving wife and two boys who were rapidly growing up into men.

Freemasonry was separating us, not only on Lodge nights, but also in the time taken to learn and rehearse the rituals as necessary. However, sense like this took me some years to discover, so let us continue whilst I can recall something of the excitement I experienced on the night when I was made an Entered Apprentice Freemason.

Chapter 18

A Review of the
Second Degree

IT seems curious to me now that I can remember little of the second degree ceremony, that of passing to the Degree of a Fellowcraft. What memories that I do retain are less horrendous than those of the first and third degrees. Perhaps I had not completely recovered from the shock of the first degree. More probable was the fact that in this degree all the Temple lights were on full and, not being hoodwinked, I could see as well as be seen and I was among newly found friends, brother Freemasons.

The various degrees in Freemasonry are kept distinct - this is why separate obligations are required at the opening of every ceremony. Thus I had been present at the initiation of another candidate at the meeting on the month following my own. Of course members are excluded from being present in the Lodge to witness a ritual which they have not "taken" personally, being admitted for the opening of the Lodge and then being asked to leave for a short time whilst the business of the next degree is enacted.

King Solomon's Temple is the focal point of the second degree. The action describes how fellowcraft Masons can enter to receive their wages. All this seemed at the time to be straight forward, simple stuff when compared to the first and third degrees. As I write quite a different idea has come to my mind.

Quoting selectively from I Kings: 11 v. 1 - 10, please bear in mind God's specific instruction to all the Children of Israel not to inter-marry with any of the indigenous people of Canaan and the surrounding countries:-

"Now King Solomon loved many foreign women along with the daughter of Pharoah; Moabite, Ammonite, Sidonian, and Hittite women from the nations concerning which the Lord had said to the sons of Israel, 'You shall not associate with them, neither shall they associate with you, for they will surely turn your heart away after their gods,' Solomon held fast to these in love. And he had 700 wives, princesses, and 300 concubines, and his wives turned his heart away. For it came about when Solomon was old, his wives turned his heart away after other gods, and his heart was not wholly devoted to the Lord his God, as the heart of David his father had been ..... And Solomon did what was evil in the sight of the Lord, and did not follow the Lord fully ..... Then Solomon built a high place for Chemosh the detestable idol of Moab on the mountain which is east of Jerusalem .... Thus he did for all his foreign wives .... Now the Lord was angry with Solomon because his heart was turned away from the Lord, the God of Israel, who had appeared to him twice, and had commanded him concerning this thing, that he should not go after other gods; but he did not observe what the Lord had commanded."

It is hardly possible to draw hard and fast con-
clusions from the above extract from I Kings. King
Solomon had received wisdom from God greater
than had been granted to any other man. Whilst he
walked with God all went well and Solomon was
blessed to such an extent that even the Queen of
Sheba exclaimed, in I Kings: 10 v.7:-

"Nevertheless, I did not believe the reports,
until I came and my eyes had seen it. And behold,
the half was not told me. You exceed in wisdom
and prosperity the report which I heard."

This being so, what was likely to happen when
such a vast intelligence lost its integrity? Would it
excel in cunning and evil? This is the course taken
by so many of King Solomon's successors. Would
it turn to the fallen Lucifer? If Solomon did consort
with Satan it would go some way to explain the
implications behind Freemasonry.

Chapter 19

A Review of the Third Degree

AS we turn to take a look at the third degree, let us review the overall pattern of the Craft Masonry. Briefly, the first degree of the Entered Apprentice is emblematical of our entry upon this our mortal world. The second refers to our life's labours and rewards. The third prepares us for our latest hour, for death and for the re-union with our former companions and fellow-workmen.

The basis of the ceremony of the third degree is the re-enactment of the story of a Master Mason, one Hiram Abiff. He is slain by unworthy workmen because he refused to share with them the secrets of his exalted degree, that is, of a Master Mason. He was slain by a blow to the head with a heavy maul - a mason's wooden hammer. In the ceremonial working, after a gentle tap on the forehead the Candidate is laid on the floor of the lodge to represent this dead Master Mason "rather indecently interred."

The story continues that when Hiram Abiff was missed search parties were sent out. When the corpse was found efforts were made to raise him by the Entered Apprentice's grip but "it proves a slip." The handgrip of the Fellowcraft "proves a slip likewise." Then a more experienced workman, by taking a more extended grip of the corpse's right hand - in the ceremony it is the Candidate's right arm which is grasped by the Worshipful Master of the Lodge - he is raised on the five points of fellowship. These may be enumerated thus if my memory serves me well:-

"Hand to hand I greet you as a brother; foot to foot, I will support you in all your laudable undertakings; knee to knee, the posture of my daily supplications will remind me of your wants; breast to breast, your secrets when entrusted to me I will guard as my own; and hand over back, I will protect your honour in your absence as in your presence."

The sentiments thus expressed seemed to me at the time to be an excellent way of declaring the concern of a Freemason for a fellow Freemason. Let us be frank about this, if all mankind applied these points to all mankind, then the world would be vastly different from what it is to-day. It is so simple to accept these maxims at their face value and miss entirely the underlying heresy.

This portion of the ceremony of being "killed" and "raised" took place for me in very reduced lighting. On being raised it was pointed out to me that even by

"this dim light I could see that I stood on the very brink of the grave into which I had figuratively descended."

I was standing on the end of a drape upon which was represented an open coffin and grave. I was then shown a skull and a couple of large bones as the emblems of mortality. All this is dramatic stuff!

and I, for one swallowed it all, hook, line and sinker, even the assurance that:-

"the light of a Master Mason's Lodge is darkness visible".

Only recently did I come to realise what this might mean, this darkness that is visible. My thoughts went back to an incident which occurred some twenty years ago, shortly after I had been delivered from the evil realms of the occult.

I was walking along one of the halls in my home at around mid-day when I saw just that, a massive "heap" of impenetrable blackness possibly eight feet tall and nearly three feet wide. This "shape" confronted me; I stopped walking and stood stationary somehow numbed, unable to move and worse still, almost unable to think! It is strange, but I cannot remember any sense of craven fear at that time. I did have a vague thought that I ought to do something and that this "vague something" was very urgent and most important. Quite what it was I could not realise, at first, but, after what seemed like ages the thought of PRAYER came so very slowly into my conscious mind, so ponderously slowly. "What was prayer?".... "What is prayer?"... "Can I pray?"... "Ought I to pray?"... "How do I pray?"... "What does one say?"... "What can I say?"... "Wasn't there a set prayer? possibly a special prayer?".... "Yes, that's it, there is a prayer that I can pray".... "But what was it?... "What is it?"... "How did it start?".... As I stood, through nearly total confusion of mind came the memory of..YES, this is it: the LORD'S prayer.....things were becoming clearer, but how did it start? I felt that I had to begin at the beginning... what was the first word....? A faint light of inspiration glowed, and then suddenly I had it! "Our Father... yes, that's it, it's coming....,"Our Father, Who art in heaven............" and as I recalled the opening words of the Divine Prayer I was lifted up out of the mental muddle and I began to think clearly and then to realise that the Darkness that had faced me had gone! Never again have I experienced such a confrontation with Evil.

"Darkness visible" - the meaning for me was now quite evident, it is Satan. The Masonic Ritual now appeared in quite a different light, sinister, threatening......

But to return to the Masonic Temple, after I had been raised from this figurative death I was allowed to leave the Lodge to "restore my personal comforts", that is to unroll my trouser legs and put on my jacket and was assured that the ceremony would be resumed upon my return.

Re-entering the Lodge I was conducted to a seat of honour in the middle of the temple facing a picture on an easel. The conclusion was an explanation of the Third Degree Tracing Board upon which is delineated a coffin, skull and bones - emblems of mortality. So here was I, alive and well, listening to a masonic lecture on the ultimate destiny of mankind after I had acted out the part of the central character in a murder "play" where the corpse had come alive again. The notion of "resurrection" did not occur to me until years later. Now it seems inescapable, that Freemasonry teaches salvation is at the hand of "a more expert workman" using the grip of a Master Mason.

In due time, with sufficient fortitude, eager members may reach the office of Worshipful Master. In most lodges of Freemasons there is a change of member occupying the "Chair of King Solomon" each year. The raising of the succession of Candidates is performed by a succession of Worshipful Masters. At no time during any of the ceremonies thus far was the idea of intervention by the Great Architect of the Universe, Grand Geometrician or the Most High, or whatever the name is that is used, ever even mentioned. Is man the means of his own salvation, the saving of his own soul? Surely this is what the first three degrees in Freemasonry lead us to conclude.

Again these questions must be faced. How can Freemasonry declare itself not to be a religion? How can it claim to have any relationship whatsoever with Christianity, as its claim is the uniqueness of Jesus Himself?

The fundamental idea of Freemasonry is that, in the final analysis, man and man alone is sufficient. Although he invokes the assistance and blessing of heaven upon the affairs of the Lodge, at no point in the rehearsals of the ritual can I perceive any opportunity or opening for divine intervention at all. Great emphasis is laid upon the antiquity of the ceremonies, with no deviations being allowed. Where then did it really all start? Where can progress enter? Where can advances be made? Where is the approach to the Most High made and how is contact and communion to be made?

Perhaps the next ceremony, that of being exalted to become a Companion of the Holy Royal Arch of Jerusalem, may shed some light.

Chapter 20

A Review of the Holy Royal Arch

IT was my experience that most Freemasons of my acquaintance took the first three degrees of Craft Masonry and then decided not to proceed with any more steps. The repetition of these ceremonies of Blue Craft Masonry month by month did not satisfy me. The friendship was tremendous, yes, but this was not solely the reason why I had sought to be made a Mason. Being a churchwarden and Sunday school teacher under a very active curate, who was also a Freemason, provided me with all the friendship I needed over and above that provided by the many friends I met during my secular employment. I was out to discover the real, genuine secrets of a Master Mason wherever the search took me. After making persistent enquiries I found my way to be invited to join a Chapter of the Holy Royal Arch of Jerusalem.

This highlights an interesting facet of Freemasonry. It is not for Masons to solicit among their friends for new members for initiation, so I was told. The onus was always to be on the outsider who had formed a favourable impression of the Brotherhood because of the behaviour of Freemasons of his acquaintance. This applies only to the first three degrees, the second and third following duly as time and opportunity permit. For all other degrees it seemed that one had to wait to be invited. In one sense I was fortunate in that a senior Mason took me under his wing and made the necessary arrangements.

In retrospect this is quite a reasonable procedure. If one was satisfied with the first three degrees then one was not likely to be keen and vigorous for Masonic ideals in the higher echelons of power.

The ceremony of exaltation commences by the candidate being blindfolded before his admittance into the Masonic Temple. When light was restored to me I was standing facing along the chapter which had been decorated with standards representing the twelve tribes of Israel. Instead of a triune leadership of Worshipful Master and the Senior and Junior Wardens situated at the east, west and south of the Lodge there were three Principals with the titles of Zerubbabel, Haggai and Joshua seated across the dais at the eastern end.

As a newly exalted Companion of the Order I was informed that, contrary to what I might have thought, I had not taken another degree in Freemasonry, as might have been supposed, but that I had just completed the third. Was I any nearer to the central Secret of Freemasonry? What was I being shown and taught in Chapter?

The basic theme of this ceremony seemed to be the rebuilding of King Solomon's Temple in the times of Ezra and Nehemiah. As the ritual maintains that the Royal Arch is the completion of the degree wherein Hiram Abiff is raised from the dead, we are dealing now with a situation of presenting imagery of life after death, the reunion of all the tribes of Israel, spiritually speaking, with their spiritual Father.

There is one very obvious way in which the third degree is incomplete, that is the question of the genuine secrets of a Master Mason. If they were known by Hiram Abiff alone, they were lost when he was killed. One of the prayers in the third degree is that heaven might aid masonic efforts to repair that loss. As a temporary expedient, certain substituted secrets, i.e., words, pass-words, referring to the death of the builder, were incorporated into the text of the ritual. Much of the burden of the Royal Arch ceremony is concerned with the re-discovery of these secrets in a subterranean room hidden under the rubble of the ruined former Temple. To-day, thinking back to the days when I was a newly exalted Companion, I am appalled with myself that I was intrigued and taken in as it were, by a rigmarole that does not stand up to examination in the light. I began to realise that Satan has spiritual force and power with which I, and indeed all mankind, have to reckon.

Towards the close of the ceremony I was taken to an "altar of incense", a double cube in the centre of the room. On the top was resting a square metal plate upon which was a circle and an inscribed triangle also of metal - the whole affair being a foot or so square and thus about two feet high. On the circle corresponding to the points of the triangle were an aleph, beth and lamedh - the A,B & L of the Hebrew alphabet. On the circle but opposite the sides of the triangle were the letters:- JE - HO - VAH, and on the three sides of the triangle were the letters:- JAH - BUL - ON. Originally made in gold and marble (so I was informed) in actual fact the altar that I was shown was made of wood painted white with the symbols made of brass.

By juggling around with these Hebrew characters expressions such as AB BAL, LAB BAL, etc. could be made. These were translated, explained to me as meaning FATHER LORD, WORD LORD, SPIRIT LORD.... but as a scholar told me later, these interpretations were not all correct.

JEHOVAH was a word I knew well as being one of the forms in which the tetragrammaton was rendered in modern English - JeHoVaH or YaHWeH - from the Hebrew YHWH, the vowels not being recorded. This name was so sacred to the Israelites that it was never uttered, Adoni (Lord) being used in its place.

Then came the revelation that the last word was the "real" name of the "TRUE AND LIVING GOD MOST HIGH" :- JAHBULON!. This, I was informed is a composite word consisting of three parts:- JAH, BUL, ON. JAH is the god of the Israelites; BUL the god of the Syrians; and ON one of the hierarchy of the gods of Egypt. As a Royal Arch Companion I was told that I must not utter this word by myself, but only in the company of, and with the help of two other Royal Arch Companions. We were each to repeat one of the syllables in turn, and each starting in turn, the word being repeated three times. I realise that this may seem puerile when seen in print, but this is what happened, to the best of my memory, when I became a Companion in the Royal Arch Degree. Thus, if JAH of Royal Arch Freemasonry is to be identified with "JAHWEH", the God of Abraham, Isaac and Jacob, then YAHWEH is on a par with BUL (Baal?) and ON (Osiris?). This conclusion is inescapable for the three Companions speak these two "names" taking one syllable each of JEHOVAH and JAHBULON in turn.

For the sake of regularity, on the night of my exaltation two experienced members joined me to show me how these two names were to be shared correctly.

The first says "JE", the second "HO", the third "VAH"; then the second starts off with "JE" and the third and first follow with "HO" and "VAH". Thus "JEHOVAH" is repeated three times; similarly with "JAHBULON". The three companions individually say:-

"JE-VAH-HO", "HO -JE-VAH", "VAH-HO-JE",

"JAH-ON-BUL", "BUL-JAH-ON", "ON-BUL-JAH."

I hope that you can realise from this that the two words are each repeated three times by syllables, with each of the Royal Arch Companions starting in turn and following round in sequence.

In the Holy Bible God, Jahweh, declares that He is a jealous God Who commands that:-

"Thou shalt have no other gods before - besides Me!" (Exodus 20 v.3).

In Isaiah 44 vv.6-8 we read:-

"Thus says the Lord, the King of Israel and his Redeemer, the Lord of hosts: 'I am the first and the last, and there is no other God besides Me. And who is like Me? Let him proclaim and declare it; yes, let him recount it to Me in order, from the time that I established the ancient nation. And let them declare to them the things that are coming and the events that are going to take place. Do not tremble and do not be afraid; have I not long since announced it to you and declared it? And you are my witnesses. Is there any God besides Me, or is there any other Rock? I know of none'."

There are other such references in the Bible which can be located by means of concordances, but in this particular text God states that He is King and Redeemer. This was written probably between 800 and 700 years before Christ, pointing forward to Jesus, His Ministry and crucifixion, resurrection, ascension and the fulfilment of His promise, Pentecost. Obviously all Christians know and accept this but what of the Freemason and the secrets of his "Masonic arts"?

Looking back at the theme of the third degree again, can it be that the candidate

"is raised from a figurative death by a companion of his former toils"

simply and solely to impress more forcibly on the candidate's mind the story of the integrity of Hiram Abiff who chose to be killed rather than betray his "sacred trust" - the genuine secrets of a Master Mason? What else can be the implication of this figurative raising from death be other than that of resurrection to salvation and everlasting bliss in the Grand Lodge above?

Regretfully I have to acknowledge that for many years I could see no incompatibility between being a Christian and a Freemason. The reason for this is now clear to me, I did not know the true meaning of the word. 'Christos' in Greek becomes 'Christ' in English by dropping the 'os' and means "the Annointed One". Similarly the diminutive form 'Christianos' becomes 'Christian', a little anointed one. The anointing of the power of God the Holy Spirit is the same as the Father conferred upon Jesus. Being blessed in this way God the Holy Spirit conveyed to me the truth.

Consider the obligations, oaths of secrecy, peculiar to each degree. They may savour of childish pranks, perhaps to be taken lightly, but adding a little zest to the evening's meeting. In fact it was suggested to me when I began to query the obligations that I should not take them too seriously. Jesus stated that it was that which came out of a man's mouth that condemned him, for a man speaks out of the fullness of his heart. What a close parallel to Adam and Eve's situation in the Garden of Eden when the tempter suggested to Eve that God had got it wrong when He said that she would die if she disobeyed His Word. Satan hasn't changed much! As God takes everything that we say with our mouths into consideration then the situation is horrific, and this with one's hands on the Bible!

Now, as Freemasonry proclaims that the Holy Bible as one of its great "Lights", then surely it should abide by its precepts. If one does accept the Holy Bible as being the Word of Almighty God, and therefore true, what of this assertion by Jesus:-

"No one comes to the Father but by Me!" (John 14 v.6)?

and this is quite categorical!

One supernatural Entity, Satan, opposed Jesus during His earthly ministry. In John: 8 v.44 we read that Jesus referring to His opponent the devil says:-

"Whenever he speaks a lie, he speaks from his own nature; for he is a liar, and the father of lies."

Jesus continuing His address to the Jews:-

"But because I speak the truth, you do not believe Me."

By studying Matthew's account of Jesus' temptations in the wilderness in the beginning of chapter 4 one can sense something of the impending tremendous battle. Such was Jesus' triumph that the author of the letter to the Hebrews in 2 v.14, 15 could write:-

"Since the children share in the flesh and blood, He Himself likewise also partook of the same, that through death He might render powerless him who had the power of death, that is, the devil; and might deliver those who through fear of death were subject to slavery all their lives".

Also, in I John: 3 v.8 we find:-

"The Son of God appeared for this purpose, that He might destroy the works of the devil."

During conversations that I have had with Freemasons there is one comment that has cropped up a number of times, namely,

"I get more from going to the Lodge than I do from attending church."

It is all too easy to rebut this for one goes to church primarily to offer worship and praise, in fellowship with other believers, to God the Father through the mediation of Jesus in the power of God the Holy Spirit. Thus churchgoing is not principally to receive but to give, but God in His infinite mercy desires to bless us more than we can comprehend, and so He showers His love upon us. The point I wish to make here is that Freemasons have compared their Lodge meetings with attendance at church. In any case they frequently refer to their place of meeting as "The Temple", sing hymns, say prayers and use the names of scriptural people as passwords. Much of the allegory of Freemasonry centres around the Temple built by King Solomon in the second degree and its rebuilding in the Royal Arch ceremony. For example, the principal characters, if I may use that term, in the latter degree take the names:- Zerubbabel, Haggai, Joshua, Ezra and Nehemiah. This being so, it is difficult to see how it can be maintained that Freemasonry is not a religion.

If its devotees insist that Freemasonry is not a religion, bearing in mind these superficial similarities, what in very truth is it? Taking a radical step and by saying that it is all of Satan, a demonic subterfuge, a counterfeit church, the way of living in the kingdom of Darkness, clarity begins to appear. The first comment that comes to my mind is that I was "hoodwinked" for so many years, seeing "truth" where no TRUTH was and where there is no TRUTH! Freemasonry considered as a counterfeit of religion makes uncommonly good sense when viewed from the vantage point of a Freed-mason!

Freemasons continue to assert that the Craft is not a religion; so, if it is not a religion - with the references to the Great Architect of the Universe, the Grand Geometrician, the True and living God Most High, JAHBULON - what can it be? The deft definition of:-

"a peculiar system of morality veiled in allegory and illustrated by symbols"

means virtually nothing to me, but it sounds reasonable.

The progression of the candidate through the four ceremonies is to represent a man's walk through life until he reaches

"that Grand Lodge above whence all goodness emanates".

All this is achieved

"by the help of God"

- whatever that may mean to a non-religious person - and by the

"assistance of more expert craftsman"

- that is, the Worshipful Master of the Lodge after the hand grips of the Entered Apprentice and the Fellowcraft have both failed.

Wherein does the power, the authority to raise the candidate from the dead reside? Is it in the grip of a Worshipful Master of a Master Mason's Lodge? Can the grip of a Master Mason raise a brother Mason from the dead so that he can attain eternal salvation? Is man the captain of his fate? If so, what becomes of his wife as she is rigidly excluded from Freemasonry? I have been informed that the ladies have developed quasi-masonic associations - for their own salvation?

Can a Christian be a Freemason?

Epilogue
and
Appendices

Epilogue

JESUS declared Himself openly as Lord and Saviour and the only Way to His Father.

The true nature of Freemasonry is hidden in mystery. May I suggest that it is a case of the blind leading the blind, degree by degree, into the web of Satanic intrigue?

Thus, the choice is entirely up to you. The decision to come to the Lord Jesus is yours and yours alone; it is solely in your own heart. There is no other way of rescue available except by the power and authority of His Name.

The actual provision of salvation is God's prerogative and is in His divine hands alone. We cannot make even a down payment on the eternal heavenly life He freely offers to us in the Name of Jesus; God for His part will never overrule the free-will that He has given to us out of the Almightiness of His Love.

"For God so loved the world that He gave His only begotten Son, that whosoever believes in Him should not perish, but have everlasting life." - John: 3 v.16.

Appendix "A"

The Relationship of Freemasonry and Religion

BEING an extract from the Report of the Board of General Purposes adopted by Grand Lodge in December, 1981.

On 12th September, 1962 the Grand Lodge adopted a statement on the relationship of Freemasonry and religion. The Board believes that it is of fundamental importance to the reputation and well being of English Freemasonry that no misunderstanding of the subject should exist in the Craft or outside it, and that it is opportune to re-issue the statement. Its text follows:

"It cannot be too strongly asserted that Masonry is neither a religion nor a substitute for religion. Masonry seeks to inculcate in its members a standard of conduct and behaviour which it believes is acceptable to all creeds, but studiously refrains from intervening in the field of dogma or theology. Masonry, therefore, is not a competitor with religion though in the sphere of human conduct it may be hoped that its teaching will be complementary to that of religion. On the other hand its basic requirement that every member of the Order shall believe in a Supreme Being and the stress laid upon his duty towards Him should be sufficient evidence to all but the willfully prejudiced that Masonry is an upholder of religion since it both requires a man to have some form of religious belief before he can be admitted as a Mason, and expects him to go on practising his religion.

"The Board hopes that Grand Lodge will agree that this is a valid statement of the Masonic position, and in the practical application of these principles will lay down:

(i) that Masonic rites, prayers and ceremonies be confined to the Lodge room, and that dispensation to wear regalia (which term includes white gloves) in public be granted only in exceptional cases;

*(ii) (withdrawn by leave of Grand Lodge)

(iii) that there be no active participation by Masons, as such, in any part of the burial service or cremation of a Brother and that there be no Masonic prayers, reading or exhortations either then or at the graveside subsequent to the interment, since the final obsequies of any human being, Mason or not, are complete in themselves and do not call in the case of a Freemason for any additional ministrations. That if it is wished to recall and allude to his Masonic life and actions, this can appropriately done at the next Lodge Meeting in the presence of his Brethren, or at a specifically arranged Memorial Service;

(iv) but that while no obstacle should be put in the way of Masons wishing to take part in any act of corporate worship, only in rare and exceptional cases should they be granted dispensation to do so wearing regalia; moreover that the order of service should in all cases be such as the officiating Minister or his superior consider appropriate to the occasion.

* This sub-paragraph dealt with the vocal music in degree ceremonies in the Board's report referred to in the previous paragraph and was put back for further consideration. A statement on the subject was adopted by Grand Lodge in March, 1963 and although still in force it is not necessary to repeat it here."

****

Comments on Appendix "A"

THIS report from the Board of General Purposes and adopted by Grand Lodge in December 1981 illustrates the ambiguity discussed briefly in chapter 16. Clearly it seems that Freemasonry wants its cake as well as eating it. If one believes in a Supreme Being then obviously it is His will and His will alone that is to be obeyed. Before anyone can abide by an edict it must, of necessity be known by that person. When the Divine Command is revealed one may not desire to comply, one may have one's own bright ideas, but observance is mandatory!

Much of the precepts of Freemasonry resemble the tenets of Humanism, except that the idea of the Great Architect of the Universe is well to the fore in the thoughts of the ardent Mason. Ardour, of itself, is not enough. This is the burden of the Bible, the saving grace of Jesus alone enables mankind to attain eternal life with Him in the presence of His Father in heaven. The decision to turn to Jesus in penitence is the responsibility of each individual and each individual alone; the provision of salvation is in the hands of Almighty God and in His hands alone.

Appendix "B"

Address by the M.W. the Grand Master

BEING an extract from the Report of the Annual Investiture of the Grand Lodge held on 25th April 1984.

The M. W. The Grand Master: Brethren, I welcome you all most warmly to Grand Lodge, and begin by congratulating those whom I have invested as this year's Grand Officers or whom I have promoted or appointed to Past Grand Rank. Both promotions and new appointments carry with them additional responsibility as well as new dignity and I wish them all good fortune as they continue or increase their efforts on behalf of the Craft.

Last year, for various reasons, I did not conduct this Investiture, but instead presided over the Quarterly Communication in March. In reviewing the Masonic Charities, I then expressed a hope that the Foundation would be able to find some means of providing assistance in cases of medical need which arise locally or otherwise cannot be dealt with at the Royal Masonic Hospital. I was glad therefore to hear in December that an Inquiry was being set up to consider how best the Foundation could provide for the medical care and assistance of Freemasons of the English Constitution and their families. I need hardly say that I look forward with keen interest to hearing what the Committee of Inquiry recommends.

Before I proceed to my main theme, I want to refer to the admirable new book "Freemasons' Hall, the Home and Heritage of the Craft" which has just been produced. I believe the authors and publishers have done full justice to this important subject and that they deserve our warm congratulations and thanks.

Brethren, you will be aware that the Craft has recently been the subject of another "exposure", this time by an author who seems to make it a speciality to attack Freemasonry. Many of his arguments are on the basis that because some Freemasons may have misused the Craft, the Craft itself is corrupt, and that because we are staunchly private, our privacy is sinister. At the same time, fresh impetus seems to have been given to renewed expositions attempting to show why Freemasonry is incompatible with Christianity and it is even reported that local authorities are debating whether membership of the Craft is compatible with local Government.

Our response was, in the traditional manner, to be largely unresponsive. This may have temporarily dampened the delight which the media seem to take in Mason-bashing - and it is remarkable how resolute but courteous refusal to comment dampens debate - but I am beginning to wonder whether our stonewalling attitude is necessarily the best for the interests of the Craft. Giving little or no information may stifle immediate interest, but it does nothing to discourage malicious speculation or to dispel unnecessary suspicion. I believe that we - and I mean in particular the Board of General Purposes as the body which recommends Grand Lodge's policy - shall need to give the matter close attention before very long.

I am not advocating a reversal of our traditional attitude and still less an active Public Relations Campaign. I believe, however, that we should do more in preparing ourselves, as I suggested here two years ago, to explain to people, who may want to know for respectable reasons, what the Craft stands for and to stress the positive aspects of what it does for the world in general and for us personally.

In this we should not simply fall back on traditional eliptic phrases, for instance explaining Freemasonry as "a system of morality": nor do we convey much by negative explanation such as saying simply that Freemasonry is not a religion, or that it prohibits political discussion in its Lodges.

How, then do we start? Logically at the beginning, explaining, that Freemasonry is a society of men which developed, perhaps historically, from the Guilds of mediaeval operative Stonemasons. Its members follow ancient principles, which I discussed in 1980 and can summarise under the well known headings. We profess Brotherly Love by treating other men charitably and as equals. We practise Relief: we care for our own (though not as a benefit society), and we care increasingly for those who are not Masons. We strive for Truth: in calling for high moral standards, hoping that we may attain them in our own lives and perhaps influence others in the same way.

What does Freemasonry do for its members and the community? I do not need to dwell on its charitable works, which I believe are well enough known and understood by us all, particularly since the publication at the end of last year of the useful booklet "Information on Masonic Charities". I think we could well emphasise however that, in context of our ancient principles, contributions to non-Masonic Charity and pastoral or practical involvement in charitable works are very important.

We can then go further and say that Freemasonry extends the family. It should introduce us to more friends, or at least to friendly acquaintances. Its Charities may be on hand to support families if their circumstances change for the worse but - like families - they cannot always help.

As to the religious aspect, we should emphasise that Freemasonry is an ally of religion and is firmly rooted in religious belief. In all our rituals and at our meals, we are reminded of the deity to whom we owe our being. It is sad, in these days of ecumenism and, in some quarters, tolerance, that it should be considered a criticism of Freemasonry that it is not specifically Christian. It will certainly help if the phrase "Freemasonry is my religion" is never uttered again: I cannot think of any words more likely to give a false impression of the Craft. We may pray, as our forebears did, more than others pray now, but the Craft does not and cannot provide any of the usual characteristics of a religion.

When we say that we profess Brotherly Love we mean that Freemasonry encourages Brethren to help each other in a charitable and generous way. We emphatically do not mean using Masonic connections for personal gain or preferment.

This leads me to the question of what Freemasonry may mean to us as individuals: having dismissed personal gain or advancement, we can best express this as enabling a man to put something into life which he might not have done if he were not a member of the Craft. In teaching teamwork to some, it may improve their confidence. Our system of government in Lodges and elsewhere teaches a useful form of discipline and a habit of submission to the authority of the Master or a majority of the brethren (and as I have indicated before our ancient ritual, meticulously performed, provides for many its own satisfaction and reward). I cannot believe that after exposure to all these influences we are not made better men and citizens.

None of this is a direct defence to our present attacks on the Craft, but by providing a positive statement it may help to disarm the suspicious. Our best defence for the future is in our own hands, Brethren - if we take care to conduct ourselves so that when anyone is said to be a member of our Ancient Institution the world may know that he is a dependable, sympathetic, fair and kindly person: a good citizen, in fact, and one concerned in a practical way for his fellow men. This ideal is not exclusively Masonic, but if we are determined to strive for it, and can find some way, as individuals, or as a Lodge or an Institution, of quietly demonstrating what we are doing, I am confident we shall find that the public view of the Craft improves, that attacks (other than by the wilfully malevolent) may become fewer and that we ourselves get even more pride and satisfaction out of belonging. We may even persuade our detractors, in the churches, local goverment and elsewhere that we have something to offer them which they need not fear or mistrust.

I am conscious that by now some of you may wonder what I call a long speech. I make no apology for dwelling upon a subject that I believe to be of profound importance to us all, at some length and I hope that what I have said will be of use in the debates which may follow.

In conclusion, on a less philosophical note, I should like to thank those who have made this afternoon's ceremony possible, and who administer the Craft and maintain this building through the year. This includes those on my right with specific duties as Grand Officers, most conspicuously the Grand Director of Ceremonies and his Deputies; the Board of General Purposes; the Grand Secretary and his office for whom this meeting is a high peak in a whole range of mountainous activities, and the largely unseen and too often unsung array of engineers, electricians, porters and cleaners who contribute to our enjoyment of Freemasons' Hall.

Finally, Brethren, my thanks to you for attending - and for your support.

Comments on Appendix "B"

APPENDIX "B" contains in full the extract that was sent to me of the address by the Most Worshipful the Grand Master. In this book I am not interested in "Mason-bashing", the term used in the Report, nor in yet another "exposure", but rather to seek for Truth. That is the Truth of God as expressed in His Love and concern for His creation and for all His creatures. As a child of the Father I desire to do what is possible to share the Grace of Jesus, to share what He has done for me and for countless others.

As I was reading this extract I was conscious of a curious sort of flashback to the time when I was a member of the Craft wherein I began to appreciate afresh the viewpoint of the Freemason sitting in his Lodge, a concept that I once shared. An air of reasonableness, an earnestness of integrity came to my mind.

"We strive for Truth: in calling for high moral standards, hoping that we can attain them in our own lives and perhaps influence others in the same way."

This precept sounds most attractive high moral standards all round, but this is not Christianity. As I continued to think, this sense of "reasonableness" persisted. It may have been a symptom of former pride, the idea that: "I/we know something that the uninitiated do not and cannot know;" "I/we know the truth because we are on the inside." So strangely strong was this remembrance that I almost began to wonder if I were wrong to be involved in a book like this.

One inescapable conclusion to be drawn from the Old Testament is that when the Children of Israel followed their own devices instead of the leading of the Lord Jehovah they landed themselves in trouble. When they recognised this and repented, turning back to God, He heard them and rescued them again and again.

Then I remembered how the Lord had rescued me from Freemasonry and the resulting completely new life that Mary and I now rejoice in together; then the deliverance of others came to mind and all my doubts disappeared. Yes, the Craft is corrupt, it is of Satan. Jesus called him the father of lies which accounts for it having such an insidious craftiness that so many well-meaning, honest and upright men are inveigled into its meshes. If salvation could have been achieved by man's own efforts, if he had been able to restore the relationship of love which existed in the beginning by his own strength, then, would Jesus have been sent by the Father and would He have allowed Himself to be crucified? If the Almighty Creator could have found another easier solution to the problem of man's fall other than Calvary would He have not used it?

Much is made of the generosity of the Freemason to his fellow Mason, the helpless and indigent within the Craft. Also he is known for liberality outside his Lodge. "Information on Masonic Charities" of 15.11.83 and "The Grand Charity of the United Grand Lodge of England" can provide some insight into the workings of Masonic philanthropy. The Secretary, The Grand Lodge Charity, 60, Great Queen Street, London, WC2B 5AZ may have further copies of these publications.

But what has Jesus to say about charity - love? In Matthew chapter 10, where it is recorded that He sent His disciples out on their first "solo missionary trip" as it were He specifically excluded money from all considerations at that time. He said quite bluntly:-

"Freely you have received, freely give."

In other words do not charge anybody when you heal them or whatever. God always gives, Jesus gave during His earthly ministry, He gave His Life a ransom for many, yet whilst walking the earth in obedience to His heavenly Father He trusted God for His daily needs.

Again,

"We can then go further and say that Freemasony extends the family. It should introduce us to more friends, or to friendly acquaintances. Its Charities may be on hand to support families if their circumstances change for the worse but - like families - they cannot always help."

At first reading this seems so plausible and credible, and a creditable way of improving one's lot here on earth especially perhaps here in U.K. where in the 1980's family life is breaking down under the attack from the powers of darkness. One Bishop told me that of the clergy in his diocese whom he knew to be Freemasons all had family problems, problems in their parish, or both. It is so easy to think that we can lift ourselves up by our own bootlaces. Mary was on the point of divorcing me when Jesus stepped in and completely saved and restored the situation when it was utterly out of my hands, our hands. Whilst not claiming like Paul to be the chief of sinners, if the Lord can clean up the mess that was my life, He can do this to the uttermost, for all families, but,

"Apart from Me you can do nothing." - John 15: 15.

An exciting facet of "life in the Spirit" being a child of God is to meet others who are also His children. It is like meeting an old friend, someone who was a bosom pal and yet we are meeting for the very first time. Our Father is the same Person and Jesus, our Redeemer is always the same, ready to save and, if we allow Him, He always succeeds!

"As to the religious aspect, we should emphasise that Freemasonry is an ally of religion and is firmly rooted in religious belief. In all our rituals and at our meals, we are reminded of the deity to whom we owe our being."

"It is sad, in these days of ecumenism and, in some quarters, tolerance, that it should be considered a criticism of Freemasonry that it is not specifically Christian."

The dictionary entry of "ecumenic" includes the definition: "belonging to the entire Christian Church". Does this imply that the continued existence of Freemasonry should be tolerated even though it is not Christian? Anyone who is a Christian should not, must not, be a member of a non-Christian Brotherhood - "You cannot serve God and Mammon" Matthew 6: 24. Is Freemasonry part of the Mammon of Unrighteousness?

What is meant by:-

"We may pray, as our forebears did, more than others pray now, but the Craft does not and cannot provide any of the usual characteristics of a religion"?

This, surely, is a "non sequitor". For me, prayer is communion, communication with God the Father mediated by Jesus in the power of the Holy Spirit and is fundamental to the Christian faith. At a prayer meeting recently reference was made to the plumb line of God's Will which illustrates the problem here. The line hangs only one way, precisely plumb, with no deviation. Members of religions other than Christianity must face all the difficulties posed by the Craft from their own various standpoints, but for Christians Jesus challenged the Pharisees of His earthly days in Matthew chapter 22: 42, saying:-

"What do you think about the Christ, whose Son is He?"

A group of Greeks, speaking to Philip, make a valid point in John 12, v.21:-

"Sir, we would see Jesus."

No one will see Jesus within the context of Freemasonry except when He comes to rescue a sinner such as I was.

Then the Most Worshipful the Grand Master voices the view of the self-sufficiency of man.

"I cannot believe that after exposure to all these influences we are not made better men and citizens."

Here the point is not that anyone should be made better in man's sight, but that God desires that we should become acceptable to Him, to be obedient to His precepts. The appraisal of one's self or one another is utterly and totally irrelevant. We must be conformed to the Father's standard and His alone; and He, realising that man, of himself, could never achieve it sent Jesus to be the way back to Himself, to the eternal glory that is heaven being in God's presence for evermore.

Obviously many more comments could be made upon this address by the M.W. the Grand Master. I am sad to say it, but it seems to be a typical Masonic pot-pourri of secrecy, pride, pseudo-religion and humanistic fellowship. Take the sentence:

"None of this is a direct defence to present attacks on the Craft, but by providing a positive statement it may help to disarm the suspicious."

What if those suspicions are well founded? I am certain that they are. Oh that the Freemason in his Lodge would recognise these "attacks" for what they really are. They are lifelines to rescue him from an appalling fate. If sitting in Lodge were as harmless an exercise as a Sunday School outing I, for one, would not be spending hours and days typing for the first time for some forty-five years trying to share the truth about Freemasonry as God is showing it to me.

Appendix "C"

The Masonic Bible

BEING description of the Bible including extracts.

A Masonic Bible has just been loaned to me. This is the first time that I have handled a copy. It is pointless for me to speculate whether I would have stayed an ardent member of my lodge for so many years if I had read and studied the various additions to the Authorised Version.

The covers are in limp blue leather, the only difference externally from an ordinary, standard edition of the Bible is the Masonic symbol of the square and compasses blocked in gold on the lower right hand corner of the front cover. Inside there are a few "family bible" style pages whereon can be inscribed the dates of one's Initiation, Passing, Raising, etc., and also the names of the Worshipful Master, his officers, witnesses plus any members and friends on each occasion. This section concludes with "A Mason's Charge" being "the rule and guide for our faith and practice." Then follows what appears to be the standard "AUTHORISED KING JAMES VERSION" printed by the Oxford University press. Finally there are four sections:-
"THE BIBLE AND MASONRY", The Oxford Bible

Concordance for Masonic Use, ILLUSTRATIONS and finally the New Oxford Bible Maps.

As they deal specifically with Freemasonry I propose to reproduce in full the "Charge" and the longer "The Bible and Masonry" in this chapter.

****

"the rule and guide for our faith and practice"

A Mason's Charge.

"MY BROTHER: Upon reflection you will remember that among the first things which you discovered in the Lodge, on being brought to light as a Mason, was a Holy Bible open upon the Altar. You were told that it is our Volume of the Sacred Law and the Great Light of the Lodge. Upon it you took your obligations as a Mason, and you were exhorted to make it the rule of your faith and your guide in the practice of Brotherly Love, Relief and Truth, which are the aims of our ancient Order.

At each step in your advancement you were reminded that the Bible is the wisest teacher of man, directing his feet to the Temple of virtue in which alone he can find liberty and peace. Words from the Bible are heard as we enter upon each of the Degrees; its truth adds lustre to every tool and symbol of the Lodge; its light is to glory of the Craft. To defend, preserve, and obey the Bible is the first duty of every Mason, from the highest officer to the humblest workman.

Wise men of every creed agree that in the Bible are to be found those truths of faith and laws of morality upon which to build an upright character. Since it is the purpose of Masonry to lead men to righteousness, it opens the Bible upon its Altars, with the injunction to all its sons to study it diligently, to learn the whole duty of man upon earth and his hope of a life hereafter; urging each to follow the light he there shall find, and as he there shall find it.

Our Craft adopts no one system of dogma, nor does it permit the discussion of sectarian issues within its Lodges; "as what never yet conduced to the welfare of the Lodge, nor ever will." Instead, it encourages each man to be steadfast in the faith his heart loves best, and to allow all his Brethren the same right. Like a mother it takes us by the hand, leads us to the Altar, and points to the open Bible - the corner-stone of our Faith.

The key-stone of our Hope - keep it as a treasure; live with it as a friend. Its truths are holy, its laws are binding, its spirit is the breath of God. Read it often; follow it honestly; trust it utterly; and learn that the duty of man is to do justly, to love mercy, and to walk humbly with his God."

****

(Before leaving this "charge" I will make but one comment. It is in no small measure true that because I have followed that last sentence seriously that I am where I am to-day - outside Freemasonry! However, let us look at "The Bible and Free-masonry" as included in the Masonic Bible, retaining the American form of spelling).

THE BIBLE AND MASONRY

The Great Light of the Lodge
By Joseph Fort Newton, Litt.D.

I

UPON the Altar of every Masonic Lodge, supporting the Square and Compasses, lies the Holy Bible.
The old familiar Book, so beloved by so many gen-
erations, is our Volume of the Sacred Law and a
Great Light of the Lodge. The Bible opens when
the Lodge opens; it closes when the Lodge closes.
No Lodge can transact its own business, much less
initiate candidates into its mysteries, unless the
Book of Holy Law lies open upon its Altar. Thus
the Book of the Will of God rules the Lodge in its
labors, as the Sun rules the day, making its work a
worship.

Nor is it strange that it should be so. As faith in
God is the cornerstone of Freemasonry, so,
naturally, the Book which tells us the highest truth
about God is its altar-light. The Temple of King
Solomon, about which the history, legends, and
symbolism of the Craft are woven, was the tallest
temple of the ancient world, not in the grandeur of
its architecture, but in the greatness of the truth for
which it stood. In the midst of ignorant idolatries
and debasing superstitions, the Temple on Mount
Moriah stood for the Unity, Righteousness, and
Spirituality of God. Upon no other foundation can
men build with any sense of security when the
wind blows and the floods descend.

140

Therein our Fraternity is wise, building its Temple square with the order of the world and the needs and hopes of men, erecting its philosophy upon faith in spiritual verity and ruling its conduct by the immutable principles of moral law. While we may not say that Masonry is a religion, in the sense that it is one religion among many, it is none the less religious in its spirit and purpose: not simply a code of ethics, but a fraternity founded upon religious faith - its teachings transfigured by the truths of faith which lie behind all sect and religions and are the exclusive possession of none. It seeks to develop moral and spiritual life, to purify thought, to refine and exalt character - in short, to build men and then make them Brothers and Builders; and to that end it takes the Bible as its Guide, Prophet, and Friend.

By the same token, our gentle Craft knows a certain secret, almost too simple to be found out, whereby it avoids the angry disputes about the Bible by which men are divided into sects. It is profoundly religious, but it is not dogmatic. The fact that the Bible lies open upon its Altar means that man must have some Divine revelation, must seek for a light higher than human to guide and govern him. But Masonry lays down no hard and fast dogma as to the nature of revelation. Nor does it attempt a detailed interpretation of the Bible. The great Book lies upon its Altar, open for all to read, open for each to interpret for himself. It is the genius of Masonry that it unites men, not upon a creed bristling with debated issues, but upon the broad, simple truth which underlies all creeds and overarches all sects - faith in God, the wise Master-Builder, for whom and with whom man must work.

For that reason, no matter how widely religious teachers may differ in their doctrines, in the Lodge they meet with mutual respect and good will. At the Altar of Masonry they learn not only toleration, but appreciation. In its kindly air of fellowship they discover that the things they have in common are greater than the things that divide. It is the glory of Masonry that it teaches Unity in essentials, Liberty in details, Charity in all things, on the ground that all just men, all devout men, are everywhere of one religion; and it seeks to remove the hoodwinks of prejudice and intolerance so that they may recognise each other and work together in the doing of good.

II

THE history of the Bible in the life and symbolism of Masonry is very interesting, and may be told in brief, if only to reveal the development of the Craft and how the Holy Book came to its place of power in the Lodge. In the Middle Ages, to go no farther back, Freemasonry was a guild of craftsmen toiling in the service of the Catholic Church - the only Church then in existence, save a few persecuted sects deemed heretical and reckoned outside the pale of the Christian community. All the guilds of the period were intensely religious, each having its patron saint, and each its festivals when candles were burned and prayers offered at a shrine.

The oldest document of Freemasonry extant, the Halliwell Manuscript - better known as the Regius Poem - dated about 1390, is definitely Catholic in its tone and teaching. Halliwell, its discoverer, held that it is such a document as a priest might have written, opening with an invocation to the Trinity and the Virgin Mary, and devoted to the religious instruction of the Craft, including the proper way to celebrate the Mass. There were, to be sure, a number of cults and schools of various kinds, within the Church and outside, devoted to occultism and different systems of symbolism, and no doubt these influenced Freemasonry to some degree; but as a whole Masons were loyal church-men, and remained so throughout the cathedral-building period.

Let it be remembered that in the Church of that time the Bible was not the supreme authority in matters of religious faith and practice. The Church, not the Book, was the court of final appeal, and this fact was reflected in the documents of Free-masonry. While the Bible is mentioned in the old Manuscripts of the Order, and had a place of honor in the Lodge as the book upon which the oath of a Mason was taken, it is nowhere referred to as a Great Light of the Lodge. In the Harleian Manuscript, dated about 1600, the obligation of an initiate closes with the words: "So help me God, and the contents of this book." In an old Ritual, of which a copy from the Royal Library in Berlin is given by Krause, there is no mention of the Bible as one of the Lights of the Lodge.

With the advent of the Reformation the whole

situation was changed. For whole peoples and a large section of the Church the scepter of religious authority passed from the Church to the Bible, and this fact was also reflected in the history of Masonry. Indeed, it is not duly realised how truly Masonry, in its modern form, was a child of the Reformation, allied, as it was, with the group of movements out of which came the freedom of the peoples. At any rate, from the time of Edward VI on, the Order of Freemasonry was emphatically Protestant in its affinities, as is shown by the invocations used in the Old Charges of the period. Naturally, in the Lodge as in the Protestant Church, the Bible became supreme, its slow elevation not unlike the elevation of the Square in our Ritual, giving basis to the faith of the Craft and color to its rites; though, as a fact, not until we reach the Rituals of 1760 do we find it described as one of the Great Lights of the Lodge.

Just what happened at the time of the "revival", or transformation, of Masonry in 1717, and in the period immediately following the founding of the Grand Lodge of England, is hard to know. The background is hazy and the records too scrappy to enable us to trace the the many influences which must have been at work, converging in the Constitutions of 1723. It was more than a revival; it was a revolution. It not only gave Masonry a new form of organisation, finding focus in Grand Lodge, but also a new attitude towards the Church - and attitude the full meaning of which was not at once realized. Some of us would give much to know what lay behind and led up to the memorable article on "God and Religion" in the Constitutions of 1723.

That is to say, just as in the Reformation the Masonic order severed its connection with Catholicism, so in 1717 it severed itself once and for all with any church, sect, or party creed, making itself henceforth independent of any particular school of theology. It proposed to unite men upon the common eternal religion in which all men agree, asking Masons, "by whatever Denomination or persuasion they may be distinguished", to keep "their particular opinions to themselves", and not to make them tests of fellowship in the Lodge, "whereby Masonry becomes the center of union, and the means of conciliating true friendship among persons that must have remained at a perpetual distance".

Only a few realized at first how far-reaching such a statement was, but by the middle of the century its meaning was discovered, with the result a rival Grand Lodge was founded in 1751, calling itself "Ancient", on the ground that the "Modern" Grand Lodge had abandoned the faith. Two rival Grand Lodges existed side by side for more than fifty years, not always without friction, but the "Moderns" finally won, disengaging Masonry from specific allegiance to any one religion, to the exclusion of all others. In the great Lodge of Reconciliation, in 1813, the universal religious character of the Order was affirmed, and the last trace of dogmatic sectarian theology vanished from the Ritual of the Craft, let us hope for ever. Naturally all this has to do with the place and influence of the Bible in Masonry, where it held an office of honor even in days of division and debate, its inherent majesty shining the brighter as sectarian obscurations were removed.

III

SO much every Mason ought to know of why the Bible lies upon the Altar of the Lodge, a source of strength, a focus of fellowship, and a symbol of the Will of God for the life of man. To-day the Holy Book is central, sovereign, supreme, the master light of all our seeing, a law to our hearts and a light to our Craft. From the Altar it pours forth upon the East, the West, the South its white light of spiritual vision, moral law and immortal hope. Almost every name in our ceremonies is a Bible name, and students have traced about seventy-five references to the Bible in our Ritual. But more important than direct references is the fact that the spirit of the Bible, its faith, its attitudes toward life, pervades Masonry like a rhythm or a fragrance.

As the Mason reads his Bible he will find many things familiar to him in Masonry, in imagery as well as in idea, aside from its fundamental spiritual faith and moral command, which are in our human world like the great rock ribs which hold the earth together. The Bible is a chamber of imagery, a book of parables, a literature of symbols, and it shows us life under many metaphors and similitudes, among them the imagery of architecture - man the builder, God the Builder, and men as living stones to be cut, polished, and built into a House of the Eternal; and we learn in a new setting the old symbolism of the working tools as we are taught to use them in the Lodge.

Yet the Mason will search the Bible in vain for anything akin to the Masonic ceremony or degree. Even in the history of the building of King Solomon's Temple - the motif of our symbolism and drama - there is nothing which resembles, or even remotely suggests, what we are shown in the Lodge. To cite but one example: the tragedy of Hiram Abiff, so central in the mysteries of Masonry, is not met with by hint or intimation in the Biblical record. Whether the people of the Bible had an esoteric teaching, or an order of initiation, we do not know. If they did not, they were in this respect unlike almost all other peoples of the ancient world. If they did, they have kept their secret so well that we have failed to find it out to this day.

Plainly the biblical coloring of Masonry - its scenery and setting to-day - did not come into it directly from the Bible, but from secondary sources and by long roundabout ways which we are unable to trace; so that by the time the Craft had taken its legendary, to say nothing of its ceremonial form, its dramas suggested by incidents in the Bible had been transformed into new shapes and put to new uses. The Legend of the Lost Word, the Substitute Word, the Great Temple, the Master Builder, all these, and much else in Masonry, no doubt had their original inspiration and suggestion directly from biblical narratives; but they have since travelled so far, passing through so many transformations, that they have wellnigh lost all touch with their sources, and, as a fact, have become a system of universal symbolism, belonging equally to all men and all religions. And that is as we should like to have it, because Masonry, alike by its principles and its profession, is seeking to create a universal fellowship.

The drama of the Master Degree, as all agree, was modelled upon the the drama of the Ancient Mysteries, a drama older than the Bible, older than the civilisation whose origin and development the Bible records and interprets. When, where, and by whom this oldest of all dramas was taken up, recast, and given its biblical setting and symbolism, nobody knows and we may never learn. Some think it was the work of Jewish Kabbalists of the Middle Ages, by whose influence and genius the Temple of King Solomon became, and remained for a long period, a center of symbolical thought and a focus of speculative philosophy. But whether it was due to the Kabbalists or not remains a mystery yet unsolved. Anyway, out of the far past the wonderful thing we call Masonry emerged, making use of biblical imagery and emblems, a system of moral mysticism, a teacher of wise and good and beautiful truth; "a way of common men to God".

No Mason needs to be told what a great place the Bible has in the Masonry of to-day. As soon as the initiate enters the Lodge, he hears Bible words recited as an accompaniment to his advance toward the Light. Upon the Bible he takes solemn vows of love and loyalty, of chastity and charity, pledging himself to the practice of the Brotherly

Life. Then as he moves from one degree to another, the imagery of the Bible becomes familiar and eloquent, and its music sings its way into his heart. In the First Degree he hears the 133rd. Psalm, in which a happy singer of a time far gone celebrates the joy of a God-anointed brotherly fellowship, as gentle as the dew descending upon Mt. Hermon. In the Second Degree he sees in the imagery of the prophet Amos a plumb-line held in the hand of God, and let down from heaven to test the worth and work of men and nations. In the Third Degree he listens to the last chapter of Ecclesiastes, a litany of old age and decay, unmatched in any language, describing the slow crumbling of mortal powers and the masterful negation and collapse of the body, until the golden bowl is broken, and the dust returns to dust, and the spirit of man takes its long last flight to the God who gave it.

When the shadow of terrifying tragedy falls over the scene of the drama, when stupid cunning seems to triumph over moral nobility, and heroic integrity is stricken down by blind brutality, leaving man dismayed and appalled, as if the high values of life were worthless and at the mercy of low force and foul crime, there is a prayer, one of the greatest in literature - a mosaic of Bible words - bitter hard in its realism to life, yet touched by the pathos of our mortal lot, and only redeemed from despair by the hope of man in God who will not let him be utterly cut off, lest something in God die too, and chaos come again, and dull death and its devouring grave be victor over all.

IV

LIKE everything else in Masonry, the Bible, so rich in symbolism, is itself a symbol - that is, a part taken for the whole. It is a symbol of the Book of Truth, the Scroll of Faith, the Record of the Will of God as man has learned it in the midst of the years - the perpetual revelation of Himself which God has made, and is making, to mankind in every age and land. Thus, by the very honor which Masonry pays to the Bible, it teaches us to revere every Book of Faith in which man has found help for to-day and hope for the morrow. For that reason, in a Lodge consisting of Jews the Old Testament alone may be placed upon the Altar, and in a Lodge in the land of Mohammed the Koran may be used, according to the laws of the mother Grand Lodge. Whether it be the Gospel of the Christian, the Book of the Law of the Hebrew, the Koran of the Mussulman, or the Vedas of the Hindu, it every-where Masonically conveys the same idea - symbolising the Will of God revealed to man, ex-pressing such faith and vision as he has found in the fellowship of seekers and finders of God.

None the less, while we honor every Book of Faith in which man has found comfort and com-mand, with us the Bible is supreme, at once the mother-book of our literature and the master-book of the Lodge. Its truth is inwrought in the symbolism of our Craft and the very fiber of our being, with whatsoever else of the good and the true which the past has given us. Its spirit stirs our hearts like a sweet habit of the blood; its vision lights all our way, showing us the meaning and the worth and destiny of life. Its very words have in them memories, echoes and overtones of voices long since hushed, and its scenery is interwoven with the holiest associations of our lives. Our fathers and mothers read it, finding in it their final reason for living faithfully and nobly, and it is thus a part of the Ritual of the Lodge and the ritual of life.

It behoves every Mason, of every rite and rank, not only to honor the Bible as the Great Light of the Craft, but to read it, study it, live with it, love it, lay its truth to heart and learn what it means to be a man. There is something in the old Book - a sense of God, a vision of moral order, a passion for purity, an austere veracity, a haunting pathos and pity - which, if it gets into a man, makes him both gentle and strong, faithful and free, obedient and tolerant, adding to his knowledge virtue, patience, temperance, self-control, brotherly love and pity. The Bible is as high as the sky and as deep as the grave; its two great characters are God and the Soul, and the story of their life together is its ever-lasting romance. It is the most human of books, telling us half-forgotten secrets of our own hearts, our sins, our sorrows, our doubts, our hopes. It is the most Divine of books, telling that God made us for Himself, and that our hearts will be restless, unhappy, and alone, until we find our rest in him whose will is our peace."

Comments on Appendix "C"

INCLUDING extracts from the Masonic Bible concordance.

Prior to commenting upon the two previous extracts which are unabridged in order to provide an unbiassed report of what Freemasonry proclaims, let us look at the note that precedes the concordance, one selected entry therein and one selected entry in the Illustrations.

****

NOTE

"THE compilation here presented of a concordance to the Bible from the Masonic point of view should be judged with the consideration accorded a pioneer effort. It might seem at first sight rather strange that nothing of the kind has hitherto been attempted, but the reason probably is that the former members of the Craft were in general thoroughly conversant with the Scriptures from earliest youth, and through this familiarity were able to bring to mind the passages that had peculiar significance to Freemasons. On all hands it must be recognised that to the present generation the Bible is largely a sealed book, even though it is open on the altar of the lodge.

It thus happens that many direct allusions to scriptural passages in the Masonic Ritual and that almost innumerable echoes of biblical language lose much of their force; so that there is need of an index giving the reference to Bible objects and figures of speech, to persons and places, of interest to Masons. The concordance offers a ready means of finding Scripture allusions to buildings and builders, to tools and implements, to symbols and allegories, adopted by, or parallel to, those familiar to the Craft, and finally to those biblical phrases and words that are used in the same or a similar sense in the Ritual.

In this last the task has proved peculiarly difficult, and there has been the constant danger on including what was not really apposite and omitting what ought to have been included. The work has been done primarily in reference to the Degrees of the Blue Lodge and the Chapter, but Cryptic Masonry and the chivalric orders and to some extent the Ancient and Accepted Scottish Rite have also been kept in view.

It is hoped that the concordance may draw the attention of the Craft, especially the younger members, to the intimate connection of the Ritual with the language of the whole Bible, and not merely to the passages definitely referred to; and, if this be accomplished, the preparation and publication of the work will have compassed worth-while objectives."

In the concordance, which is entitled "For Masonic Use", under the general heading of the entry on "LIFE" there is a section:-

"Eternal, the gift of God through Jesus Christ (Ps 133.3); Mat 20. 28; John 6. 27, 54; 10. 28; 17. 3; Rom 2. 7; 6. 23; 1 John 1. 2; 2. 25; Jude 21; Rev 2. 7; 21.6."

and then follows a sub-section:-

"to whom promised. Mat 10. 39; John 3. 16; 5: 24; 1 Tim 1. 16."

****

Now to the "Illustrations" which contains twelve pages of text plus twenty full page line drawings. Plate III refers to:-

"The Procession of the Ark:- Amen-hetep III, king of Egypt, offering incense before the ark of Amen-Ra."

(Please note that this does not refer to the ARK of Jehovah. This entry is included to indicate the general content of "Illustrations" which is solely concerned with the history and the archeological aspects of Egypt, Assyria and Babylonia. There is no reference to the early history of the Jews that I have discovered. - Ed.)

****

Returning to the contents of the previous chapter, in "A Mason's Charge" reference is made to the Holy Bible being open on the ALTAR. What is an "altar"? My dictionary has a number of definitions, but the basic import in them all is:-

"a block or table for making sacrifices on."

Now what is the sacrifice that is being made

during Masonic ceremonies? This is a very good question, one to which I had not addressed myself until this very moment, which we must consider straightaway.

There is no problem now for me over the sacrifice of Jesus at Calvary. I was a sinner, Jesus was sinless, the Perfect dying and paying all the debts incurred by my transgressions for all time as I stay in communion with the Lord and repent of any misdemeanour as soon as I receive the revelation of it. Thanks be to God Who gives me, and all Christians, the victory in Christ Jesus.

However, what is the offering being made in Freemasonry? Basically, apart from possibly T.G.A.O.T.U., (The Great Architect of the Universe) only two characters are involved in the ceremonies, the Worshipful Master and the Candidate. The Master is certainly making no personal sacrifice during the meeting, he is ruling his Lodge. He, assisted by his officers, is leading the new member through the successive stages of Freemasonry, through a further step in his Masonic career. Each degree in Freemasonry demands another obligation, all the various degrees are to be kept separate. Thus, do the brethren in Freemasonry consider that in taking these solemn vows the candidate is in fact making something of a sacrifice? If so, what is it? The penalties of the various obligations, as far as those of which I am aware are concerned would, unquestionably, have fatal results if literally carried out, executed. If a sacrifice is being made, is it the life, spiritual life of the candidate that is being offered? If so, to whom? Certainly it isn't to Jehovah, the God of the Holy Bible, for in His Word it is abundantly clear that He has accepted the sacrifice of His only begotten Son, Jesus - see, for example, Hebrews: 9 v. 11 onwards.

The only other person interested in the souls of men is Satan. Vowing, swearing, with one's hands on the Volume of the Sacred Law, only compounds the crime for, in the Sermon on the Mount - Matthew: 5 v.33 onwards - Jesus forbids absolutely the swearing of oaths. Should this then be the case that the Masonic obligation is an offering to Satan, then it ties in with all my other thoughts about the Institution. It explains at least to some extent why it is that whole families are affected by the man's membership of a demonically based organisation. Isn't it a piece of superb trickery and cunning to exhort the newly initiated and obligated Freemason to "make it (the Bible) the rule of your faith"?

Certainly Satan isn't above using such a subterfuge for he presumed to quote the Scriptures to Jesus during His temptations in the wilderness (Mat 4 v.6). Such is the authority of Holy Writ that Jesus Himself refuted Satan with further quotations from the Old Testament; the point being that Jesus had permisson and authority to do so in the power of the Holy Spirit whose anointing He had just received. To-day it is still true that it is only with the power of Holy Spirit available from the Father through the mediation of Jesus that anyone can be rescued from occult Freemasonry.

Where is the "Temple of virtue" to which the

candidate's feet are directed? Have all Freemasons found the "liberty and peace" contained therein?

There is much in "A Mason's Charge" that is almost true. Take the first sentence of the third paragraph:-

"Wise men of every creed agree that in the Bible are to be found those truths of faith and laws of morality upon which to build an upright character."

but the point is that the Bible contains examples and ample proof that man, of himself, cannot attain the suggested rectitude, certainly not the state of righteousness desired by Almighty God. Time after time the Israelites of old failed to such an extent that at one time Elijah thought he was the only one left who was still faithful to the God of the Israelites (I Kings 19: v.14). Does the Freemason in his Lodge think that he can do better? God in His infinite wisdom realised that salvation, restoration of man, required something greater - the sacrifice of His only Son!

"Since it is the purpose of Masonry to lead men to righteousness, it opens the Bible upon its Altars";

but the real aim of God's Word is to lead His children to Him, to a personal relationship with Jesus who is alive to-day having been raised from the dead.

"It encourages each man to be steadfast in the faith his heart loves best and to allow his brethren the same right."

And that is a heap of pernicius nonsense if you like! The fundamental point of Original Sin in the

Garden of Eden is "I know best!" Yet Jesus calls His disciples, now as well as then, to bear witness to Him! Bear in mind that the Bible records Jesus as saying that He was the only Way.

"Like a mother it takes us by the hand, leads us to the Altar, and points to the open Bible - the corner-stone of our faith."

Has the person who wrote this ever read the Bible himself?

"Its laws are binding....."

but Jesus came to set free all the sinners who came to Him. To be truly a Christian is to be truly set free by the grace of Jesus in the love of the Father by the power of the Holy Spirit! The Christian lives by the grace of faith and not under bondage to the Law.

Now let us turn to "The Bible and Masonry". The first sentence:-

"Upon the Altar of every Masonic Lodge supporting the Square and Compasses, lies the Holy Bible"

contains the implication that the Square and Compasses are of more significance than the Bible. Having a Bible - or any other book - open in Lodge or Temple is of no significance at all unless the thoughts and edicts contained on the pages are shared, unless it is read. As Mr.J.F.Newton states in section IV the Koran or Vedas might be supporting the Square and Compasses and the thoughts expressed in these books are not identical, and neither agrees with the claims of the Bible. The presence of the Bible open when the Lodge is open and closed when the Lodge closes savours more of magic than anything else. Much is made of the use of the Temple of King Solomon as a symbol of the Unity, Righteousness and Spirituality of God; yet God allowed it to be destroyed. It was rebuilt in the times of Ezra and Nehemiah certainly, but it was completely flattened, not one stone upon another, in A.D.70 by the Romans as foretold by Jesus Himself; what happened to God's Unity, Righteousness and Spirituality? Carrying this allegory one stage further, God reveals to John, who records the vision in Rev. 21 v.2, that He is going to provide the New Jerusalem. What can man do towards that project? Nothing, for it comes down out of heaven.

"Our Fraternity is wise, building its Temple square with the order of the world ...... immutable principles of moral law."

One can doubt the wisdom of this statement for the words of Jesus are completely opposite; His disciples are not of this world.

"Our gentle Craft knows a certain secret, almost too simple to be found out."

Did Jesus have any secrets? He shared all that the Father had told Him, indeed the very words He uttered were not His but the Father's.

In part II we read:-

"of the Catholic Church - the only Church then in existence save a few persecuted sects deemed heretical and reckoned to be outside the pale of the Christian community."

No doubt the Pharisees and Sadducees viewed Jesus in the same sort of light. They were the leaders of their day, the Sanhedrin, and Jesus was the interloper upsetting the organised way in which they "ran" the Temple worship. There is no possibility of misunderstanding their condemnation by Jesus' epithet of "whited sepulchres." Could modern Masonry be considered pharisaical?

Were the guilds in the early days of Freemasonry "intensely religious" because they burned candles and prayers were offered at a shrine? Where in the Bible are the instructions to burn candles and employ shrines? Where are we instructed to include invocations to the Virgin Mary in the "proper way to celebrate the Mass"? These comments are not directed towards any denomination, but are made because I do not know any specific commands authorising them contained in the Bible, the book the Freemasons are claiming as one of the Great Lights of their Craft.

"In the Reformation the Masonic order severed its connection with Catholicism, so in 1717 it severed itself once and for all with any church, sect, or party creed, making itself henceforth independent of any particular school of theology."

In the above quotation are Freemasons claiming that they are all right - and everybody else is out of step? Jesus states that His sheep know His voice and will follow Him, yet all references to Him by name are excluded from all Lodge meetings, rituals and discussions. The fact that, apart from "Jesus", Biblical names are used for their ritual characters' titles is neither here nor there, nor is the fact that some ceremonies draw upon Scriptural situations for their substance or embellishment.

In section III it is admitted that the tragedy of

Hiram Abiff, so central to the mysteries of Masonry is not found anywhere in the Bible. In other words the story of the murder of the Master Mason is unscriptural, and it surely is permissible now to wonder whether it and all the rest of Freemasonic Ritual is simply fiction.

As the Craft does not acknowledge Jesus as Saviour and Lord, one must pose the question:-

"Where is Freemasonry leading its protagonists?

Central in section III is the observation that if the people of the Bible had no "esoteric teaching" then they were unlike virtually all the rest of the nations of their day. As one reads the Bible the fact that the children of Abraham were unusual, unique, is clear.

"The drama of the Master Degree, as all agree, modelled upon the Ancient Mysteries, a drama older than the Bible............where and by whom this oldest of all dramas was taken up, recast, and given its biblical setting and symbolism, nobody knows .....".

One trait that puzzled me when first I was made a Mason was the stress laid upon antiquity. The Lodge that accepted me is one of the oldest in English Masonry, number 114. This was a source of pride for all members to be part of such a long established Lodge. Whilst I remained a member I know I enjoyed sharing this privilege. But here it is being asserted that Freemasonry antedates the Bible itself. As the Craft claims that the Bible is a "Great Light in Freemasonry", and thus I assume that they would consider it to declare the truth, how can anybody or anything predate:-

"In the beginning God created the heaven and the earth." (Gen.I v.1)?

Other witnesses have shared with me the dual standards that they have encountered during day to day steps that they have made in their Masonic career. Is this surprising when here at the beginning of all things the facts are being "cooked". There is nothing hidden in these observations that I am being guided to make. They are there for all to see unless Satan has blinded the eyes of Freemasons. When I rang Rev. Charles "A" when the Lord told me:-

"Not to-night!"

and he had told me of the appalling dangers that I had been courting in spiritism, I still remember vividly his reply when I asked why he had not told me about it before:-

"Would you have listened?"

To-day I would have to admit that I do not think that I would have done so then.

Continuing to quote:-

"Anyway out of the far past the wonderful thing we call Masonry emerged, making use of biblical imagery and emblems, a system of moral mysticism, a teacher of wise and good and beautiful truth; 'a way of common man to God.'"

and that says much to me, for "making use" of scriptural terms for any other reason than for proclaiming the Word of God is meretricious.

The penultimate paragraph of section III concludes:-

"the spirit of man takes its long last flight to the God who gave it."

with not the slightest suspicion of a hint of the saving grace of Jesus or the Day of Judgement. Perhaps reference ought to be made to the closing chapters of the Bible. What does Revelation:20 v.11 - 15 for example tell us?

"And I saw a great white throne and Him who sat upon it, from whose presence earth and heaven fled away, and not place was found for them.

And I saw the dead, the great and the small, standing before the throne, and books were opened; and another book was opened, which is the book of life; and the dead were judged from the things which were written in the books, according to their deeds.

And the sea gave up the dead which were in it, and death and Hades gave up the dead which were in them; and they were judged, every one of them according to their deeds.

And death and Hades were thrown into the lake of fire. This is the second death, the lake of fire.

And if anyone's name was not found written in the book of life, he was thrown into the lake of fire."

In the closing paragraph of section IV is written:-

"There is something in the old Book - a sense of God, a vision of moral order, a passion for purity, and austere veracity...."

and there seems no comment needed to amplify that quotation.

As with virtually everything connected with

Freemasonry, section IV continues to be so plausable, so reasonable:-

"None the less, while we honor every Book of Faith in which man has found comfort and command, with us the Bible is supreme..."
but this is not what Jesus maintained. He repeatedly stressed His uniqueness, that He was the only Way to the Father, and that we who had accepted Him as Saviour and had become children of God, should not be yoked with unbelievers - see II Cor. 6 v.14:-

"Do not be bound together with unbelievers; for what partnership have righteousness and lawlessness, or what fellowship has light with darkness?"

Thus Christians are not to honour other beliefs nor other Books of Faith. If this makes one think that Christianity is an exclusive faith, that is right for it is so. Jehovah is a jealous God, but He is love and loves His creation. Everyone who responds to His call is accepted in the Beloved, in Jesus!

In the closing sentences we read:-

"The Bible is as high as the sky and as deep as the grave; its two great characters are God and the Soul, and the story of their life together is its everlasting romance."

What does this mean? A romance can often be the product of someone's fanciful imagination; is this poetic fiction? The LIFE that God has designed for us, for which mankind was created, transcends all earthly limits. These are Satan's domains at the moment. The grave is not part of the inheritance of the Christian for his Lord has conquered death in all its aspects. The truth that the Bible declares is that God desires man to return to Him. So great is His desire and love that He provided the way, the only Way possible, in and through belief in His Beloved Son.

This is for me the amazing aspect of Freemasonry that it can refer its members to texts such as John 3. 16, and yet continue to rehearse their rituals of Entering, Passing and Raising - Birth, Living and Death & Resurrection. I reproduce this verse as it is in the Masonic Bible.

"For God so loved the world, that he gave his only begotten Son, that whosoever believeth in him should not perish, but have everlasting life."

The Bible, especially the New Testament, proclaims that Jesus of Nazareth is the Son of God, His Christ, His Annointed One. If the Freemason is obedient to the commands of his Lodge, operating under the Constitutions of the United Grand Lodge of England, which uses the Bible as its Volume of the Sacred Law, he cannot fail to study the passages that are listed above. If he does so in all honesty he is faced with a dichotomy. How can this dilemma be resolved? The Craft maintains the principle of good works, being raised at the hands of a "more expert workman". The Bible maintains that salvation is the free gift of God through the perfect sacrifice of His Son, Jesus the Christ. Both cannot be right!

Appendix "D"

What is Freemasonry

BEING a copy of a pamphlet produced by the Board of General Purposes of the United Grand Lodge of England.

INTRODUCTION

FREEMASONRY is one of the world's oldest secular fraternal societies. This leaflet is intended to explain Freemasonry as it is practised under the United Grand Lodge of England, which administers Lodges in England and Wales and in many places overseas. The explanation may correct some misconceptions.

Freemasonry is a society of men concerned with moral and spiritual values. Its members are taught its precepts by a series of ritual dramas, which follow ancient forms and use stonemasons' customs and tools as allegorical guides.

THE ESSENTIAL QUALIFICATION FOR MEMBERSHIP

THE essential qualification for admission into and

continuing membership is a belief in a Supreme Being.

Membership is open to men of any race or religion who can fulfil this essential qualification and are of good repute.

FREEMASONRY AND RELIGION

FREEMASONRY is not a religion, nor is it a substitute for religion. Its essential qualifications opens it to men of many religions and it expects them to continue to follow their own faith. It does not allow religion to be discussed at its meetings.

THE THREE GREAT PRINCIPLES

FOR many years Freemasons have followed three great principles:

Brotherly Love
Every true Freemason will show tolerance and respect for the opinions of others and behave with kindness and understanding to his fellow creatures.

Relief
Freemasons are taught to practise charity, and to care, not only for their own, but also for the community as a whole, both by charitable giving, and by voluntary efforts and works as individuals.

Truth
Freemasons strive for truth, requiring high moral

standards and aiming to achieve them in their own lives.

Freemasons believe that these principles represent a way of achieving higher standards in life.

CHARITY

FROM its earliest days, Freemasonry has been concerned with the care of orphans, the sick and the aged. This work continues today. In addition, large sums are given to national and local charities.

FREEMASONRY AND SOCIETY

FREEMASONRY demands from its members a respect for the law of the country in which a man works and lives.

Its principles do not in any way conflict with its members' duties as citizens, but should strengthen them in fulfilling their public and private responsibilities.

The use by a Freemason of his membership to promote his own or anyone else's business, professional or personal interests is condemned, and is contrary to the conditions on which he seeks admission to Freemasonry.

His duty as a citizen must always prevail over any obligation to other Freemasons, and any attempt to shield a Freemason who has acted dishonourably or unlawfully is contrary to this prime duty.

SECRECY

THE secrets of Freemasonry are concerned with its traditional modes of recognition. It is not a secret society, since all members are free to acknowledge their membership and will do so in response to inquiries for respectable reasons. Its constitutions and rules are available to the public. There is no secret about any of its aims and principles. Like so many other societies, it regards some of its internal affairs as private matters for its members.

FREEMASONRY AND POLITICS

FREEMASONRY is non-political, and the discussion of politics at Masonic meetings is forbidden.

OTHER MASONIC BODIES

FREEMASONRY is practised under many independent Grand Lodges with standards similar to those set by the Unitied Grand Lodge of England.

There are some Grand Lodges and other apparently masonic bodies which do not meet these standards, e.g. which do not require a belief in a Supreme Being, or which allow or encourage their members as such to participate in political matters. These Grand Lodges and bodies are not recognised by the Unitied Grand Lodge of England as being masonically regular, and masonic contact with them is forbidden.

CONCLUSION

A Freemason is encouraged to do his duty to his God (by whatever name he is known) through his faith and religious practice; and then, without detriment to his family and those dependent on him, to his neighbour through charity and service.

None of these ideas is exclusively Masonic, but all should be universally acceptable. Freemasons are expected to follow them.

Published by the Board of General Purposes
of the
Unitied Grand Lodge England.
FREEMASONS' HALL
GREAT QUEENS STREET
LONDON, WC2B 5AZ.
1984.

Comments on Appendix "D"

THERE is no question mark in the title so presumably this is a statement of the potentials of the Craft as seen by their experts. In it they continue to tread the impossibly narrow path between demanding the belief in a Supreme Being as a necessary qualification for initiation and the blunt assertion that Freemasonry is not a religion. Nor is it, they continue to assert, a substitute for religion. The late Dr. C.E.M. Joad who, when asked a question, frequently responded by asking in return:-

"Well, It all depends on what you mean by ....?"

What do they mean by a Supreme Being? What is religion in their view? What dictionary do Freemasons use? Humpty Dumpty in "Through the Looking Glass" by Lewis Carroll should prove an acceptable bed-fellow for he quite openly made words mean what he wanted them to convey for "he paid them well!"

As regards "brotherly love", since I resigned from the Craft this has been very conspicuous by its absence with a few notable exceptions. In "truth" to aim for high moral standards is indeed praiseworthy. The Bible says that without divine aid, faith, it is impossible to attain any morality which is acceptable to God (Hebrews: 11 v.6). This is the purpose of the writing of this book. No one can receive eternal life, the Kingdom of God, without the mediation of Jesus.

Financial aid features prominently in the pattern of Freemasonry's plan of charity. This can be of great assistance, but the Greek word "charisma" whence this word stems has a much wider connotation. Indeed, in modern translations of the Bible the last verse in I Corinthians: 12 renders "faith hope and charity" as "faith hope and love". If we look at the earthly life of Jesus, we find that throughout His ministry in Palestine some two thousand years ago, financially He lived from day to day solely in His Father's provision. When He was asked for the tribute money Peter had to go fishing (Matthew 17: vv.24-27); He had nowhere to lay His head (Matthew 8: v.20). Yet when five thousand were hungry He fed them (Matthew 14: vv.19-21)!

Even if Freemasonry's principles do not in any way conflict with a member's duty in society, there is ample evidence in the public press that society has a different point of view. This reaction may be initiated in suspicion and fuelled by ignorance but recent attempts to remedy this situation, such as this present pamphlet, are singularly inept. If Freemasonry demands respect for the law from its members, not all members of the Law are in agreement with the Craft. See for example chapter 13.

In the paragraph about "secrets" it is admitted that Freemasonry has classified information in addition to the various modes of recognition. From one point of view the outsider might not be able to care less what they are, but as someone who has been rescued from the Craft I am deeply concerned for those I have left behind and who are still hood winked. The thought of discovering and exercising those Masonic Arts which would be revealed to me in due time had spurred me on. Where would they have led me? The ritual indicates "from this sub-luminary abode to the Grand Lodge Above whence all goodness emanates." This is in direct contradiction to the Bible, to Christianity. The Bible, in I John: 1 vv 5,6,7, we read:-

"And this is the message we have heard from Him and announce to you, that God is light, and in Him there is no darkness at all.

If we say that we have fellowship with Him and yet walk in the darkness, we lie and do not practice the truth;

but if we walk in the light as He Himself is in the light, we have fellowship with one another, and the blood of Jesus His Son cleanses us from all sin."

and again in Ephesians 5 v.11:-

"And do not participate in the unfruitful deeds of darkness, but instead even expose them;"

Freemasonry does not accept the divinity of Jesus Christ. At the same time it embraces men of many religions and expects them to continue the exercise of their individual faiths at the same time as they continue to sit in Lodge; believers forced to sit with unbelievers - from the Christian point of view.

Having expressed that in my opinion Free-masonry is satanic in essence, it now occurs to me that the Brotherhood could be part of the prepara-tion of the way for the world-wide church of the Anti-christ which is featured in the Bible as a sign of the "last days". Freemasonry takes pride in its antiquity, sometimes spelling "antient" with a "t", but how old is it? There are not many lodges in this country that are more ancient than two centuries. Thus, despite the use of Old Testament themes and characters' names in the various ceremonies, it is a comparatively modern movement. I wonder why Freemasonry ever developed, but especially why in these days? Are these the Last Days of this Dispensation?

It is interesting to note that there are Grand Lodges which are not recognised by the United Grand Lodge of England and from which English Freemasons are barred, instancing lack of belief in a Supreme Being and/or political activity as the reason. But who makes these judgements? and by whose standards and authority? Man's morals in these days of video nasties are utterly useless!

In the conclusion the floodgates are really flung wide open!

"A Freemason is encouraged to do his duty first to his God (by whatever name he is known) through his faith and religious practice;..."

God, my heavenly Father is a jealous God Who is particular about His Name. He told Moses that it was:-

"I AM THAT I AM",

the ever eternal Present. In Exodus: 20 v7 He states that we are not to take His Name in vain. On the other hand Jesus gave His permission to His disciples and followers to use His NAME with His full authority. There is no other Name given among men whereby we must be saved. As I am a Christian, a born-again believer, a little annointed one, this is my confession.

Appendix "E"

Constitutions of the United Grand Lodge of England

BEING a description of and extracts from the Book of Constitutions 1940.

Recently, whilst chatting with a friend who is also a Freemason, the question of the the book of the constitutions of the craft arose. It transpired that he had more than one copy and he offered me a choice. I selected the 1940 edition, for this was the one that had been issued to me when I first was made a Mason.

It is a small, pocket-size book some four inches by five and of some two hundred pages containing a Sanction, summary of Antient charges, Charges of a Freemason and then the General Laws and regulations for the government of the Craft. After the comprehensive index there is a Appendix of engravings of Jewels, Chains and Collars. A "Queen's Regulations" of Freemasonry sums up the idea well.

The Laws and Regulations occupy ninety percent of the book and deal with the basic problems that could possible face Worshipful Masters and Masons in the conduct of their Lodges. In the preliminary twenty pages or so the dichotomy of

Freemasonry is presented, but I must confess that I did not see it when I was a Freemason. Reading these pages to-day I am amazed that I was so blind in those days. In the belief that it may be of help I propose to reproduce these Charges in full.

Page i carries the Sanction:-

UNITED GRAND LODGE OF ENGLAND

United Grand Lodge
having approved of this Revised Edition of the Book of the Constitutions, the Board of General Purposes have accordingly superintended its publication.

(signed) Sydney A. White
G.S.

Freemasons' Hall, London.

Summary of the ANTIENT CHARGES AND REGULATIONS to be read by the Secretary (or acting Secretary) to the MASTER ELECT, prior to his Installation into the Chair of a Lodge.

----

1. You agree to be a good Man and true, and strictly obey the moral law.

2. You are to be a peaceable Subject, and cheerfully conform to the laws of the country in which you reside.

3. You promise not to be concerned in plots or conspiracies against Government, but patiently to submit to the decisions of the Supreme Legislature.

4. You agree to pay a proper respect to the Civil Magistrate, to work diligently, live creditably and act honourably by all Men.

5. You agree to hold in veneration the original Rulers and Patrons of the Order of Free-Masonry, and their regular successors, supreme and subordinate, according to their Stations; and to submit to the Awards and Resolutions of your Brethren in general Lodge convened, in every case consistent with the Constitutions of the Order.

6. You agree to avoid private piques and quarrels, and to guard against intemperance and excess.

7. You agree to be cautious in your carriage and behaviour, courteous to your Brethren, and faithful to your Lodge.

8. You promise to respect genuine and true Brethren, and to discountenance Impostors and all Dissenters from the original Plan of Free-Masonry.

9. You agree to promote the general good of Society, to cultivate the Social Virtues, and to propagate the knowledge of the Mystic Art as far as your influence and ability can extend.

10. You promise to pay homage to the Grand Master for the time being, and to his officers when

duly installed, and strictly to conform to every Edict of the Grand Lodge.

11. You admit that it is not in the power of any Man or Body of Men to make innovation in the Body of Masonry.

* see footnote.

12. You promise a regular attendance on the Communications and Committees of the Grand Lodge, upon receiving proper notice thereof, and to pay attention to all the duties of Free-Masonry upon proper and convenient occasions.

13. You admit that no new Lodge can be formed without permission of the Grand Master or his Deputy, and that no countenance ought to be given to any irregular Lodge, or to any person initiated therein; and that no public processions of Masons clothed with the Badges of the Order can take place without the special Licence of the Grand Master or his Deputy.

14. You admit that no person can regularly be made a Free-Mason or admitted a Member of any Lodge without previous notice and due enquiry into his character; and that no Brother can be advanced to a higher Degree except in strict conformity with the Laws of the Grand Lodge.

15. You promise that no Visitor shall be received into your Lodge without due examination, and producing proper Vouchers of his having been initiated in a regular Lodge.

At the conclusion the Installing Officer addresses the Master Elect as follows:-

"Do you submit to and promise to support these Charges and Regulations as Masters have done in all ages?"

Upon his answering in the affirmative the Ceremony of Installation proceeds.

----

* footnote:-

(Number 11 presents a poser if taken to the limit. If NO man can make any changes to the established rituals etc., then the question must be raised:- "Whence Freemasonry?" It cannot be from the God of the Holy Bible Who sent His Son Jesus to pay the debts of the sins of all mankind. Also we read below in III - Of LODGES that "persons made masons or admitted to a lodge must be good and true men." By whose standards are these "masons" judged? - Ed.)

The title page of the Book of Constitutions follows on next in the Masonic handbook:-

THE
CHARGES
OF A
FREE-MASON:
EXTRACTED FROM
THE ANTIENT RECORDS OF LODGES
BEYOND SEA,
AND OF THOSE IN
ENGLAND, SCOTLAND AND IRELAND,
for the use of Lodges,
TO BE READ
AT THE MAKING OF NEW BRETHREN, OR
WHEN
THE MASTER SHALL ORDER IT.

Published by Order of the Grand Lodge.

with:-
THE GENERAL HEADS OF THE CHARGES OF A
FREE-MASON, &c., &c.

I. Of God and Religion.
II. Of the Civil Magistrate, supreme and
subordinate.
III. Of Lodges.
IV. Of Masters, Wardens, Fellows, and
Apprentices.
V. Of the Management of the Craft in Working.
VI. Of Behaviour

1. In the Lodge while constituted.
2. After the Lodge is over and the Brethren not gone.
3. When Brethren meet without Strangers, but not in Lodge.
4. In presence of Strangers not Masons.
5. At Home and in the Neighbourhood.
6. Towards a strange Brother.

CHARGES
OF A
FREE-MASON,
ETC.,ETC

I.-Concerning GOD and RELIGION.

A MASON is obliged, by his tenure, to obey the moral law; and if he rightly understand the art he will never be a stupid atheist nor an irreligious libertine. He, of all men, should best understand that God seeth not as man seeth; for man looketh at the outward appearance, but God looketh to the heart. A mason is, therefore, particularly bound never to act against the dictates of his conscience. Let a man's religion or mode of worship be what it may, he is not excluded from the order, provided he believe in the glorious architect of heaven and earth, and practise the sacred duties of morality. Masons unite with the virtuous of every persuasion in the firm and pleasing bond of fraternal love; they are taught to view the errors of mankind with compassion, and to strive, by the purity of their own conduct, to demonstrate the superior excellence of the faith they may profess. Thus masonry is the centre of union between good men and true, and the happy means of conciliating friendship amongst those who must otherwise remained at a perpetual distance.

II.-Of the CIVIL MAGISTRATE, SUPREME AND SUBORDINATE.

A MASON is a peaceable subject to the civil powers, wherever he resides or works, and is never to be concerned in plots and conspiracies against the peace and welfare of the nation, nor to behave himself undutifully to inferior magistrates. He is cheerfully to conform to every lawful authority; to uphold, on every occasion, the interest of the community, and zealously promote the prosperity of his own country. Masonry has ever flourished in times of peace and been always injured in war, bloodshed and confusion; so that kings and princes, in every age, have been much disposed to encourage the craftsmen on account of their peaceableness and loyalty, whereby they practically answer the cavils of their adversaries and promote the honour of the fraternity. Craftsmen are bound by peculiarities to promote peace, cultivate harmony, and live in concord and brotherly love.

III.-Of LODGES.

A LODGE is a place where free-masons assemble to work and to instruct and improve themselves in the mysteries of the antient science. In an extended sense it applies to persons as well as to place; hence every regular assembly or duly organised meeting of masons is called a lodge. Every brother ought to belong to some lodge, and be subject to its by-laws and the general regulations of the craft. A lodge may be either general or particular, as will be best understood by attending it, and there a knowledge of the established usages and customs of the craft is alone to be acquired. From antient times no master or fellow could be absent from his lodge, especially when warned to appear at it, without incurring a severe censure, unless it appeared to the master and wardens that pure necessity hindered him.

The persons made masons or admitted members of a lodge must be good men and true, free-born, and of mature and discreet age and sound judgement, no bond-men, no women, no immoral or scandalous men, but of good report.

IV.-Of MASTERS, WARDENS, FELLOWS and APPRENTICES.

ALL preferment among masons is grounded upon real worth and personal merit only; that so the lords may be well served, the brethren not put to shame, nor the royal craft despised; therefore no master or warden is chosen by seniority, but for his merit. It is impossible to describe these things in writing, and therefore every brother must attend in his place, and learn them in a way peculiar to this fraternity. Candidates may, nevertheless, know that no master should take an apprentice unless he has sufficient employment for him; and, unless he be a perfect youth, having no maim or defect in his body that may render him incapable of learning the art, of serving his master's lord, and of being made a brother, and then a fellow-craft in due time, after he has served such a term of years as the custom of the country directs; and that he should be descended of honest parents; that so, when otherwise qualified, he may arrive at the honour of being the warden, and then the master of the lodge, the grand warden and at length the grand master of all the lodges, according to his merit.

No brother can be a warden until he has passed the part of a fellow-craft, nor a master until he has acted as a warden, nor grand warden until he has been master of a lodge, nor grand master unless he has been a fellow-craft before his election, who is also to be nobly born, or a gentleman of the best fashion, or some eminent scholar, or some curious architect, or other artist descended of honest parents, and who is of singularly great merit in the opinion of the lodges. And for the better, and easier, and more honourable discharge of his office, the grand master has the power to choose his own deputy grand master, who must then be, or have formerly been, the master of a particular lodge, and who has the privilege of acting whatever the grand master, his principal, should act, unless the said principal be present, or interpose his authority by letter.

These rulers and governors supreme and subordinate, of the antient lodge, are to be obeyed in their respective stations by all the brethren, according to the old charges and regulations, with all humility, reverence, love and alacrity.

N.B.- In antient times no brother, however skilled in the craft, was called a master-mason until he had been elected into the chair of a lodge.

V.-Of the MANAGEMENT of the CRAFT in WORKING.

ALL masons shall work honestly on working days, that they may live creditably on holy days; and the time appointed by the law of the land, or confirmed by custom, shall be observed.

The most expert of the fellow-craftsmen shall be chosen or appointed the master, or overseer of the lord's work; who is to be called master by those that work under him. The craftsmen are to avoid all ill language, and to call each other by no disobliging name, but brother or fellow; and to behave themselves courteously within and without the lodge.

The master, knowing himself to be able of cunning, shall undertake the lord's work as reasonable as possible, and truly dispend his goods as if they were his own; nor to give more wages to any brother or apprentice than he really may deserve.

Both the master and the masons receiving their wages justly, shall be faithful to the lord, and honestly finish their work, whether task or journey; nor put the work to task that hath been accustomed to journey.

None shall discover envy at the prosperity of a brother, not supplant him, nor put him out of his work, if he be capable to finish the same; for no man can finish another's work so much to the lord's profit, unless he be thoroughly acquainted with the designs and draughts of him that began it.

When a fellow-craftsman is chosen warden of the work under the master, he shall be true both to master and fellows, shall carefully oversee the work in the master's absence, to the lord's profit; and his brethren shall obey him.

All masons employed shall meekly receive their wages without murmuring or mutiny, and not desert the master till the work be finished.

A younger brother shall be instructed in working, to prevent spoiling the materials for want of judgment and for increasing and continuing of brotherly love.

All the tools used in working shall be approved by grand lodge.

No labourer shall be employed in the proper work of masonry; nor shall free-masons work with those that are not free, without an urgent necessity; nor shall they teach labourers and un-accepted masons as they should teach a brother or fellow.

VI.-Of BEHAVIOUR.

1.-IN THE LODGE WHILE CONSTITUTED.

YOU are not to hold private committees, or separate conversation, without leave from the master; nor to talk of anything impertinently or unseemly, or interrupt the master or wardens, or any other brother speaking to the master; nor behave yourself ludicrously or jestingly while the lodge is engaged in what is serious and solemn; not use any unbecoming language upon any pretence whatsoever, but to pay due reverence to your master, wardens and fellows, and put them to worship.

If any complaint be brought, the brother found guilty shall stand to the award and determination of the lodge, who are the proper and competent judges of all such controversies (unless you carry them by appeal to the grand lodge), and to whom they ought to be referred, unless a lord's work be hindered in the meanwhile, in which case a particular reference may be made, but you must never go to law about what concerneth masonry, without an absolute necessity apparent to the lodge.

2.-BEHAVIOUR AFTER THE LODGE IS OVER, AND THE BRETHREN NOT GONE.

YOU may enjoy yourselves with innocent mirth, treating one another according to ability, but avoiding all excess, or forcing any brother to eat or drink beyond his inclination, or hinder him from going when his occasions call him, or doing or saying anything offensive, or that may forbid an easy and free conversation; for that would blast our harmony, and defeat our laudable purposes. Therefore no private piques or quarrels must be brought within the door of the lodge, far less any quarrels about religion, or nations, or state policy, we being only, as masons, of the universal religion above-mentioned; we are also of all nations, tongues, kindreds, and languages, and are resolved against all politics, as what never yet conduced to the welfare of the lodge, nor ever will.

3.-BEHAVIOUR WHEN BRETHREN MEET WITHOUT STRANGERS, BUT NOT IN LODGE FORMED.

YOU are to salute one another in a courteous manner, as you will be instructed, calling each other brother, freely giving mutual instruction, as shall be thought expedient, without being overseen or overheard, and without encroaching upon each other, or derogating from that respect which is due to any brother, were he not a mason; for though all masons are, as brethren, upon the same level, yet masonry takes no honour from a man that he had before; nay, rather it adds to his honour, especially if he has deserved well of the brotherhood, who must give honour to whom it is due, and avoid ill manners.

4.-BEHAVIOUR IN PRESENCE OF STRANGERS, NOT MASONS.

YOU shall be cautious in your words and carriage, that the most penetrating stranger shall not be able to discover or find out what is not proper to be intimated; and sometimes you shall divert a discourse, and manage it prudently for the honour of the worshipful fraternity.

5.-BEHAVIOUR AT HOME AND IN YOUR NEIGHBOURHOOD.

YOU are to act as becomes a moral and wise man; particularly not to let your family, friends, and neighbours, know the concerns of the lodge, &c., but wisely consult your own honour, and that of your antient brotherhood, for reasons not to be mentioned here. You must also consult your health by not continuing together too late or too long from home after lodge hours are past; and by avoiding gluttony and drunkeness, that your families be not neglected or injured, nor you disabled from working.

6.-BEHAVIOUR TOWARDS A STRANGE BROTHER.

YOU are cautiously to examine him in such a method as prudence shall direct you, that you may not be imposed upon by an ignorant, false pretender, whom you are to reject with contempt and derision, and beware of giving him any hints of knowledge.

But if you discover him to be a true and genuine brother, you are to respect him accordingly; and if he is in want you are to relieve him if you can, or else direct him how he may be relieved. You must employ him some days, or else recommend him to be employed. But you are not charged to do beyond your ability; only to prefer a poor brother that is a good man and true before any other poor people in the same circumstances.

Finally.-All these charges you are to observe and also those that shall be communicated to you in another way; cultivating brotherly love, the foundation and cope-stone, the cement and glory, of this antient fraternity, avoiding all wrangling and quarrelling, all slander and backbiting, not permitting others to slander any honest brother but defending his character and doing him all good offices, as far as is consistent with your honour and safety, and no farther. And if any of them do you an injury, you must apply to your own or his lodge at the quarterly communication, as has been the antient laudable conduct of our forefathers in every nation; never taking a legal course but when the case cannot be otherwise decided, and patiently listening to the honest and friendly advice of master and fellows, when they would prevent you from going to law with strangers, or would excite you to put a speedy period to all lawsuits, that so you may find the affair of masonry with more alacrity and success; but with respect to brothers or fellows at law, the master and brethren should kindly offer their mediation, which ought to be thankfully submitted to by the contending brethren; and if that submission is impracticable, they must, however, carry on their process, or lawsuit, without wrath or rancour (not in the common way), saying or doing nothing which may hinder brotherly love and good offices to be renewed and continued, that all may see the benign influence of masonry, as all true masons have done from the beginning of the world, and will do to the end of time.

Amen, so mote it be.

Comments on Appendix "E"

IT was as a Freemason when I first read the "CONSTITUTIONS" of the United Grand Lodge of England. At that time I thought it to be a fair and useful basis for Freemasonry as an association of men. The extracts here reproduced are as far as possible in the original style.

The book of the "CONSTITUTIONS" of the UNITED GRAND LODGE OF ENGLAND, 1940 begins with a reproduction of its Arms facing the title page. The motto is "AUDI VIDE TACE" which can be translated:- "Listen, Look, Be Silent".

However, to read it now I am amazed at what I did not see then. How can a Christian, filled with the love and the knowledge of Almighty God keep silent? Jesus Himself told His disciples that they were to be His witnesses - and that does not mean that silence is to be maintained either in our praise and worship to Almighty God or in our sharing of His truth with each other. Nowhere are we told to be silent unless one considers not casting pearls before swine in this category, but even here the overriding commands are to love God with all our might and strength and our neighbour as one's self. There are more ways than one of bearing witness but certainly speech is one of them. To-day, in the closing quarter of the twentieth century, we who are His disciples have the privilege and responsibility to continue to bear witness to

Saviour and Lord. Here at the very beginning of our their "Constitutions" is the command to do the one thing that the Sanhedrin of 1950 years ago was unable to enforce on the first Christians. It reminds me of the triumphal entry of Jesus into Jerusalem on Palm Sunday. When He was told to tell His supporters to silence their cries of "Hosanna", Jesus replied that if they were quietened then the very stones would cry out. See Luke 19: v.39,40; also Peter and John in Acts: 4. v.19,20.

Above the escutcheon there is a possible representation of the ARK OF THE COVENANT of the Old Testament surmounted by some Hebrew characters which may be rendered :-

"Kadosh L (possibly) Jehovah."

the "possibly" being necessary for this is the unpronounced Name of God for which the Jew substitutes "Adoni" - the Lord. Actually only the consonants are printed - yodh, he, waw and he; J.H.W.H.

This can be translated:-

"Holy - or Holiness - to God."

Here right at the beginning of the book is the first indication that Freemasonry is not straight forward. What does the term "holy" mean? - "set apart" - set apart for the service of God, to do His good pleasure. Oh yes, it is all right to ascribe holiness to Adoni, for in the Bible in Leviticus: 19 v.1,2 God tells Moses to be holy for He is holy. Thus the Freemason is setting himself apart for the service of the Lord God of Israel. As the Craft, in my opinion, does not even begin to achieve this

194

objective has provided the burden for this book.

Let us look at the first charge of a Freemason concerning his relationship with God. He is not to go against the dictates of his conscience, yet the Bible tells us that in God's sight the heart of man is desperately wicked (Jeremiah: 17 v.9). Undeniably there are wicked men - and women - in the world to-day. How do their consciences fare? Are they wicked because they are not following their hearts or is it that their thoughts are different from the compilers of "Constitutions"? For myself I prefer to seek and to be led by the Holy Spirit of God. What good does it do to view the errors of mankind with compassion when, in Jesus, God has pro-vided a way of dealing with them all? Let us never forget that Jesus Himself, when addressed as "good" Master, refused the description and said that only God was good; and also promised that He would be with His sheep for ever and would never be separated from them.

In III.- Of Lodges is stated that no women or immoral men may be admitted into Freemasonry. The Gospel record states that Jesus came to save sinners, so presumably Freemasons are above the need of redemption.

What of the qualifications for the office of Grand Master as listed in the second paragraph of section IV in a fellowship that suggests that, with adequate merit, then advancement is to the top? Is the Brotherhood saying that all its members are born equal, but that some are more equal than others?

Section V concludes with a passing fair description of the modern trade union concept of the "closed shop".

Comments about section VI could begin by asking who is a "lord" and what is "a lord's work"? Obviously from the context the Lord Jesus Christ is not meant, nor, would I suggest, any human living person. Plurality of "lords" is implied. What is there left for us to select? Demons? This could be so. This is an appalling conclusion, but it does fit in with my experiences of the Craft.

Jesus proclaims His Father as loving and caring for all His children, a truly family Person. In section VI and paragraph 5 the Freemason is told:-

"particularly not to let your family, friends and neighbours, know the concerns of the lodge, &c,"

This is damning indeed, for if Freemasonry is the way of ascent from

"this subluminary abode to the Grand Lodge Above"

what of the married Mason's wife and children? left out in the cold or condemned to the fires of hell? There can be no doubt for the Freemason that he is to be separated from his family! Is this compatible with an Almighty God Who sent His Son to pay the debt for the sins of the whole world?

Paragraph 6 exhorts the Freemason:-

"to prefer a brother that is a good man and true before any other poor people in the same circumstances".

- no comment. Finally-

"that all may see the benign influence of masonry, as all true masons have done from the beginning of the world, and will do to the end of time."

Is this meant to be serious? .. or is it just idle rhetoric? .. Genesis I v.1:-

"IN THE BEGINNING GOD......."

**For a full list of other Sovereign World books
please write to:**

PO Box 17, Chichester, West Sussex PO20 6RY,
England

PO Box 329, Manly, New South Wales 2095,
Australia

PO Box 24086, Royal Oak, Auckland, New Zealand

14 Balmoral Road, Singapore 1025